WALK FREELY

EMBRACING THE LIFE CHRIST DIED FOR

JOHN P. MARTIN

Published by John Martin
Cary, North Carolina
walkfreelytoday.com

ISBN: 979-8-234-02227-1

Editing and interior layout by Anitra M. Elmore of Orchard Scribe

Printed in the United States of America

To my incredible wife, Rachel:
Your unwavering love, support, and faith have been my anchor. Your quiet strength, wisdom, and radiant spirit inspire me daily.

To my children, Victoria, Noah, and Lily:
You are living reminders of God's grace and purpose. May you always walk boldly in the freedom Christ has won for you.

To my extended family and friends:
Thank you for your love, encouragement, and prayers throughout every step of this journey.

To every reader walking this path—whether stumbling or sprinting—this book is for you. May these words stir your heart, ignite your faith, and lead you into a deeper, freer life with Jesus. We're all on this journey together, growing, learning, and becoming more like Him.

Let's keep walking freely.

TABLE OF CONTENTS

FOREWORD

Walk Freely is a book every Christian should read. For years, I lived in bondage to a performance-based view of Christianity. My friend John Martin beautifully captures the life-changing principles of discovering our true identity in Christ and experiencing the grace and freedom of the Holy Spirit.

Through vivid illustrations and practical examples, John guides believers who may be struggling to find joy in their walk with God. This book shows us how to embrace the freedom God has given and how to live fully in that freedom every day.

Dave Pridemore
Founder & President of Camp Grace, Roswell, Georgia

INTRODUCTION

So if the Son sets you free, you will be free indeed.
—John 8:36

What does it mean to be free in Christ? Is it a feeling? A future hope? A theological truth tucked away in Scripture but far from our everyday experience? For many believers, the idea of freedom can feel beautiful but distant. We sing about it. We quote scripture about it. Yet in daily life, we often live as though we are still bound by guilt, fear, comparison, addiction, shame, sin, pressure, and the heavy weight of our past.

This book was born out of a simple but powerful question: *What does it really mean to walk freely in Christ?*

I grew up in church. I was there on Sunday mornings, Sunday evenings, midweek Bible study, revivals, all of it. I was raised with a deep reverence for God and a sincere desire to live right. Yet somewhere along the way, I found myself quietly struggling under the weight of expectations I could never seem to meet. There was an unspoken pressure to perform, to be holy, spotless, and unwavering. Though the intention may have been noble, I began to confuse God's holiness with harshness.

There was a constant tension between my human frailty and the lofty standard of religious tradition. I loved God, but I lived with an undercurrent of fear—fear of not being good enough, falling short, or being exposed as spiritually weak. So I tried harder. I avoided asking questions, ignored my weariness, and hid my broken places, not realizing that I was drifting further away from the very freedom Jesus died for me to have.

Over the past two decades, I've had the privilege of walking alongside people from all walks of life. Some were broken, some were searching, and some were faithful but stuck. No matter where they were on their journey, I found the same common thread: the desire for genuine freedom. They were not seeking the freedom the world offers, which is rooted in self-indulgence or empty independence. They were searching for the freedom that Jesus promises, including freedom from sin, shame, fear, the weight of our past, and even the opinions of others. That's where **Walk Freely** began to take shape.

This book is more than a title. It's a declaration and a call to shed the burdens we were never meant to carry, and step into the grace and purpose God has prepared for us. It's about learning to move differently, by faith, not fear; by truth, not lies; by identity, not insecurity.

Each chapter unpacks a dimension of the freedom Christ offers. We'll begin by defining what true biblical freedom is and confronting the false versions we often settle for. From there, we'll walk through the ways Christ's freedom reaches into our hearts, habits, relationships, and destiny. Along the way, you'll encounter biblical truth, vivid illustrations, personal reflection, and guided questions designed to help you not just understand freedom, but live in it. Take time to carefully consider the response questions at the end of each chapter, using the included Notes pages or your personal journal for prayerful reflection.

This journey is intentionally structured for both personal devotion and small-group use. Whether you're reading privately with a journal in hand or exploring it with fellow believers, my prayer is that the Holy Spirit would breathe life into these pages and fresh revelation into your soul.

Walk Freely was born from the slow, grace-filled unraveling of legalism, shame, and striving. Its message grew as I began to encounter the heart of God, not just as Master, but as Father; not just as Judge, but as Redeemer. This work is the fruit of years of preaching, praying, pastoring, and personal wrestling. It's a journey I've walked, and now it's a pathway I'm offering to you, not as a manual of perfection, but as a guide for discipleship, spiritual formation, and community transformation.

True freedom always leads somewhere. It leads us deeper into our relationship with Jesus, further into holiness, and forward into eternal life. This is a discipleship journey that calls us to grow, to let go, to rise up, and to surrender.

You have been set free. Now let's walk it out, together.

With grace and gratitude,
John P. Martin

1

FREEDOM DEFINED

It is for freedom that Christ has set us free. Stand firm, then, and do not let yourselves be burdened again by a yoke of slavery.
—Galatians 5:1

Before we explore what it means to walk freely, we need to understand why freedom is central to the Christian life and how we are actually invited into it. To see that clearly, we must look to the One who walked in perfect freedom—Jesus Christ.

While on earth, Jesus moved with a quiet confidence, unshaken by public opinion, unmoved by fear, and untouched by shame. There was no pretense in Him, no need to prove anything to anyone. He was not hurried, anxious, or weighed down by the misguided expectations of others. He knew He was the beloved Son of the Father, and He walked freely based on that identity.

Jesus lived in total submission to the Father's will, yet He exercised total authority on earth. That is the paradox of true freedom: it is surrender and strength in perfect harmony.

He was free to touch the untouchable, dine with sinners, speak truth to power, and rest in storms. He did not flinch when the religious elite challenged Him (John 8). He stood calmly before Pilate while facing crucifixion, declaring, "You would have no authority over me at all unless it had been given to you from above" (John 19:11 ESV). That's the kind of authority true freedom produces.

In the wilderness, Jesus was tempted by the devil after forty days of fasting. Though weak in body, He remained unwavering in spirit. He resisted every temptation not by arguing, defending Himself, or relying on willpower, but by standing firmly in who He knew He was. Each time the enemy tried to twist the truth or lure Him into doubt, Jesus responded with the words, "It is written," quoting Scripture to anchor Himself in what God had already spoken (Matthew 4). His freedom came from knowing and trusting the truth, not from trying to prove anything.

In Gethsemane, He surrendered to the Father's will, not out of defeat, but devotion. Even on the cross, stripped, beaten, and abandoned, He remained free. He chose to lay down His life. No one took it from Him (John 10:18).

Jesus is the epitome of freedom, not because He avoided suffering, but because He never lost Himself in the midst of it. And now, He invites us into that same freedom.

> And He died for all, so that all those who live might live no longer to and for themselves, but to and for Him Who died and was raised again for their sake...Therefore if any person is [ingrafted] in Christ (the Messiah) he is a new creation (a new creature altogether); the old [previous moral and spiritual condition] has passed away. Behold, the fresh and new has come!
>
> —2 Corinthians 5:15, 17 (AMPC)

What Is Freedom in Christ?

This freedom that Christ died for us to have isn't about autonomy. It's about identity. It's about knowing who we are in Christ and living into that truth without reservation.

> ***Freedom in Christ is the power to live in alignment with God's will, without the chains of sin, shame, fear, or condemnation. It is freedom from the tyranny of our old nature and liberty to walk as new creations.***

Paul's words in Galatians 5 help us understand this:

> It is for freedom that Christ has set us free. Stand firm, then, and do not let yourselves be burdened again by a yoke of slavery.
>
> —Galatians 5:1

In ancient times, a yoke was a large, heavy wooden beam fitted across the shoulders of two oxen, used to bind them together so they could plow a field or pull a heavy load. It forced both animals to move in the same direction and at the same pace. Tight leather straps fastened it around their necks, making it impossible for them to turn freely or act independently. The yoke symbolized burden, submission, and control. It determined:

- Where the oxen could go
- When they could rest
- What pace they had to move at
- And most importantly, who they belonged to

So when Paul says, "Do not let yourselves be burdened again by a yoke of slavery," he's not just warning against sin. He's confronting anything that pulls us back into performance-based religion, fear, shame, or legalism and anything that causes us to relate to God through obligation instead of intimacy.

The Better Yoke: Freedom with Christ

Now contrast that with Jesus' invitation in Matthew 11:

> Come to Me, all you who are weary and burdened, and I will give you rest. Take My yoke upon you and learn from Me, for I am gentle and humble in heart, and you will find rest for your souls. For My yoke is easy and My burden is light.
>
> —Matthew 11:28-30

This is one of the most freeing paradoxes of the Christian life: Jesus offers us a new kind of yoke, one that doesn't weigh us down, but lifts us up. It's a yoke that doesn't enslave, but aligns, and it doesn't demand perfection, but invites restful partnership.

To walk freely doesn't mean we walk alone or without guidance. It means we now walk with Christ, side by side, led by grace, learning from the One who is gentle and humble in heart. In His yoke, we find not only direction, but delight.

So when Paul pleads with the Galatians not to return to the yoke of slavery, he's calling them (and us) to remember that we've already been offered something far better: A yoke that leads to rest, renewal, and true identity. We're not free to carry *nothing*; we're free to carry something lighter and far more beautiful.

The enemy doesn't mind you believing in Christ, as long as you still live like a captive. But Christ didn't just set you free on paper—He gave you access to a whole new way of living.

Freedom Is Not a Feeling—It's a Realization

Ultimately, God's concept of freedom begins with a shift in perception. It's not about whether we feel free. It's about who declares us free, and whether we trust the One who does.

This framework reveals the nature of our spiritual freedom:

1. Freedom is **pronounced** by someone with authority over you.
2. Then it's **announced** to you.
3. It must be **professed** by you, even if your life doesn't yet reflect it.
4. It's **acknowledged** by others.

Let's consider the example of a prisoner serving time for crimes he committed. His legal release starts with the governor's signature. He becomes legally free even before he hears about it. Then, the news travels through the proper channels: the warden, the officers, and finally, the prisoner himself. Even then, he must accept the truth and walk out of the prison gate. His transformation becomes visible only after he chooses to walk in the footsteps of what has already been done. This is our story in Christ.

Freedom is not just something we grow into—it's something we wake up to. We are like the prisoner whose freedom has been signed, sealed, and delivered long before we feel it. The work was finished at the cross. The resurrection is our announcement. And when we believe, we begin to walk out what heaven has already declared.

In Christ, we are no longer defined by our past. Our sins no longer condemn us. We are no longer bound to perform for God's approval. Instead, we are loved, accepted, called, and new.

Freedom from the Inside Out

This is not spiritual hype, it's spiritual truth. And it's the foundation for the rest of this journey. We are free from sin's penalty and free from shame's grip. We are free to walk in purpose, to live in intimacy with God, and to stand firm when life gets hard.

Freedom doesn't mean we do whatever we want. It means we're now empowered to do what's right, to obey with joy, to surrender with peace, and to love without fear.

And yes, it's a process. Like the released prisoner, we carry habits and mindsets that don't change overnight. But just because you feel stuck doesn't mean you are stuck.

The door is open.

The chains are broken.

The invitation is real.

Now it's time to walk.

Reflection Questions

1. How do you define freedom? How has that shaped your relationship with God?

2. What does the "yoke of slavery" look like in your own life?

3. Do you tend to wait for a feeling before taking a step of faith? How can you shift your mindset to trust God's declaration over your situation?

4. What would it look like to live truly free in Christ?

5. What practical steps could you take this week to begin walking in the freedom Christ has already declared over you?

Notes

2

FREEDOM FROM SIN

Therefore, there is now no condemnation for those who are in Christ Jesus, because through Christ Jesus the law of the Spirit who gives life has set you free from the law of sin and death.
—Romans 8:1-2

What does it mean to be free from sin? For some, it conjures the impossible: a life of perfection, one where mistakes are never made again. For others, it sounds like a theological concept, attainable in heaven but out of reach on earth. And yet, the Scriptures make it clear that freedom from sin is not just a future hope, it's a present reality for those who are in Christ Jesus.

But to truly walk in this freedom, we must understand what we've been freed from, what we've been freed for, and what kind of life this freedom invites us into.

Sin: Our Old Master

Sin is more than just bad; it's a spiritual dominion. Before Christ, we were not just people who sinned; we were under the rule and law of sin. It governed our decisions, shaped our desires, and held us captive to its consequences. Paul calls this "the law of sin and death." Like gravity, it pulls us downward toward selfishness, destruction, and separation from God. But through Christ, another law has taken over. It is the law of the Spirit who gives life.

This isn't simply a legal acquittal; it's a spiritual transfer. We have been moved from one kingdom to another. From bondage to liberty, from guilt to grace. This shift changes everything, but it also raises an important question. If we have truly been set free, why do so many of us still live as though we are condemned?

Condemnation vs. Conviction

There are two words we will encounter often as we learn to walk in freedom: conviction and condemnation. They may sound similar, but they lead in entirely different directions. Understanding the difference between them is essential because one draws us closer to God, while the other pushes us away from Him.

Paul writes, "Therefore, there is now no condemnation for those who are in Christ Jesus" (Romans 8:1). Condemnation is the verdict of guilt and punishment. It declares that a person is unworthy, beyond repair, and deserving of rejection. When condemnation speaks, it does not simply point out wrongdoing. It defines the person by it. Its message is final and crushing: you are guilty, and there is no way back.

Many believers live under this weight, even after coming to Christ. Condemnation keeps us focused on our failure and trapped in shame. It drives us into hiding and convinces us that God is distant, disappointed, or angry. This voice does not come from God.

Conviction, however, sounds very different. Jesus described the work of the Holy Spirit this way: "When He comes, He will convict the world concerning sin and righteousness and judgment" (John 16:8). Conviction is not a sentence handed down from a judge. It is an invitation from a loving Father. Conviction exposes what is wrong, not to destroy us, but to restore us.

Conviction says, "This doesn't reflect who you are now. Come back to the truth. Come back to the light." It brings clarity without shame and correction without rejection. Where condemnation pushes us away from God, conviction draws us toward Him.

Condemnation is the voice of the enemy. Conviction is the gentle and faithful work of the Holy Spirit. When we confuse the two, we live like prisoners standing in front of open doors, afraid to step into freedom because we believe we are still under a death sentence. But in Christ, the verdict has already been rendered. We are no longer criminals standing before a harsh judge. We are sons and daughters welcomed by a loving Father.

Willful Sin vs. Weakness

Freedom from sin doesn't mean we'll never struggle again. It doesn't mean we become sinless. Instead, it means we're no longer enslaved to sin.

There's a difference between willful rebellion and weakness in need of grace.

- Willful sin is a deliberate decision to reject God's will and walk in disobedience.
- Weakness is a struggle we're surrendering to God, trusting His Spirit to help us overcome.

The call of Christ is to deny ourselves, take up our cross, and follow Him. This requires intentional surrender and daily self-denial. It's not legalism—it's love. We don't resist sin to earn God's love; we resist sin because we've been loved beyond comprehension.

Paul reminds us:

> Do you not know that if you continually surrender yourselves to anyone to do his will, you are the slaves of him whom you obey…
>
> —Romans 6:16 (AMPC)

In verse 18, he goes on to say we've been set free from sin and have become servants of righteousness. We serve a new Master who forgives, restores, and empowers.

When Sin Entered the World

To truly understand the freedom Christ offers, we must first grasp the weight of what we were freed from. Sin didn't start with a violent act or a public scandal; it began in a garden, through a whispered lie and a quiet decision.

In Genesis 3, Adam and Eve walked in perfect communion with God. There was no shame, no fear, no hiding, only intimacy, trust, and unbroken fellowship. But the moment they chose to believe the serpent over their Creator, everything changed. That single act fractured creation.

Innocence was lost.

Separation began.

Fear entered.

Hiding followed.

Adam and Eve once walked with God in the cool of the day, but after they chose to sin, they hid from Him among the trees. They covered themselves with fig leaves, symbolizing what humans have done ever since: mask guilt with performance, religion, or denial.

> …for when you eat from it you will certainly die.
>
> —Genesis 2:17

God wasn't bluffing when He said this to them. The result of sin is death, and not just physical death, but spiritual disconnection from the Source of life.

> For the wages of sin is death, but the gift of God is eternal life in Christ Jesus our Lord.
>
> —Romans 6:23

This is what makes the grace of Christ so radical. We weren't just misled, we were dead. We weren't just broken, we were bound. And yet, Jesus entered our fallen story, took on our curse, and died our death so we could be restored.

This is the backdrop against which the beauty of grace shines brightest. When we see how devastating sin truly is (not just in behavior but in identity), we begin to understand just how powerful freedom really is.

The Gravity of Sin and the Magnitude of Grace

We must never forget the seriousness of sin. It cost Jesus everything. The cross is not a casual symbol. It is the place where the full weight of sin collides with the full power of love. Jesus bore our punishment, carried our shame, and broke the curse of death once and for all. To minimize sin is to cheapen grace. To ignore grace is to remain in bondage.

But when we grasp the depth of our depravity and the height of His mercy, we begin to walk not just free, but humbled, thankful, and transformed.

The Prisoner's Next Steps

Think of the prisoner we introduced earlier. Legally, he has been declared free. The papers have been signed. The debt has been canceled. But in his mind, he still feels unworthy, still wears the uniform of his old life, and still hesitates at the threshold of the prison gates. Freedom has been pronounced, announced, and delivered, but it must also be embraced.

Some of us are just like that prisoner. We have been set free by the blood of Jesus, but we're still carrying the shame of what we did or who we used to be. We are still defining ourselves by old labels and failures and still believing that God is disappointed in us. But the voice of Christ echoes louder: "It is finished." The door is open. The way is clear. Now, we must walk forward, not as criminals, but as citizens of grace.

Reflection Questions

1. How do you distinguish between conviction and condemnation in your spiritual life?

2. Are there areas where you've allowed guilt or shame to keep you from embracing Christ's freedom?

3. In what ways have you struggled with willful sin versus areas of weakness that need surrender?

4. How does viewing sin through the lens of the cross increase your appreciation for God's grace?

5. What would it look like for you to walk boldly like the prisoner finally stepping into the light of freedom?

Notes

3

FREEDOM TO APPROACH GOD

In Him and through faith in Him we may approach God with freedom and confidence.
—Ephesians 3:12

Can you imagine standing in the presence of the One who created the galaxies? The God who spoke light into existence, who stretched out the heavens like a curtain, who sculpted the mountains and tells the oceans how far they can go. He is not just powerful—He is holy. Unapproachable in glory. Surrounded by unending praise.

The angels in His presence don't even look directly at Him. They cover their faces and cry, "Holy, holy, holy is the Lord Almighty; the whole earth is full of His glory" (Isaiah 6:3). This God, whose voice shakes the wilderness and whose throne is established in righteousness, invites us to come near. That's the miracle of the gospel.

When Our Feelings Keep Us from Approaching God

Even after we're saved, many of us carry a sense of spiritual distance. We hesitate to come to God unless we feel like we've been "doing better" lately. We subconsciously measure how worthy we feel to pray, to worship, to be heard. Have you ever thought something like:

- "I can't pray right now because I've messed up too much this week."
- "I need to clean myself up before I come back to God."
- "I'll talk to Him once I feel more spiritual."

That mindset is not freedom. It's the mentality of a spiritual orphan, and it stands in the way of our intimacy with God.

Free to Draw Near

When Jesus died on the cross, something extraordinary happened. Matthew records that "the curtain of the temple was torn in two from top to bottom" (Matthew 27:51). This was not a minor detail or symbolic poetry. It was a powerful declaration from God that everything had changed. To understand why this mattered so much, we need to understand what that curtain was.

In the Jewish temple, a thick, richly woven curtain separated the Holy Place from the Most Holy Place, also known as the Holy of Holies (Exodus 26:31-33). This inner sanctuary represented the dwelling place of God's presence on earth. Only the high priest could enter it, and he could do so only once a year on the Day of Atonement after offering a sacrifice for the sins of the people.

The curtain was not just decorative; it was a divine boundary, a visible reminder that sin separates humanity from God's holiness. To cross it without permission was to invite death.

When the curtain was torn at the moment of Jesus' death, it was God Himself who tore it. Tearing it from top to bottom, not bottom to top, sent a clear message that the separation had ended, the barrier was gone, and God was no longer keeping His people at a distance. Because of Christ's perfect sacrifice, what was once limited to one man, one day a year, is now accessible to all who belong to Him. We now have permanent, direct access to God.

You don't have to go through a priest.

You don't have to wait until Sunday.

You don't have to "earn" His ear.

> Let us then approach God's throne of grace with confidence, so that we may receive mercy and find grace…
>
> —Hebrews 4:16

Invited Into the King's Presence

In ancient Persia, no one could approach the king without being summoned—not even his own wife. To enter his inner court uninvited was to risk death. The penalty was absolute unless the king extended his golden scepter in mercy.

When Queen Esther learned that her people were in danger, she made the bold decision to approach King Xerxes, fully aware of the risks that lay ahead. She prayed, fasted, dressed in royal robes, and stepped into the throne room.

> When he saw Queen Esther standing in the court, he was pleased with her and held out to her the gold scepter that was in his hand. So Esther approached and touched the tip of the scepter.
>
> —Esther 5:2

Esther was received, not because she earned it, but because the king chose to show her favor.

Now imagine this: You and I serve the King of Kings, who is infinitely more holy than Xerxes, infinitely more just, infinitely more powerful. And yet we don't come trembling in fear. We don't wait outside the gates wondering if He'll grant us access. In Christ, the scepter is already extended. He has made a way for us to come boldly, not as beggars, but as beloved.

Living as God's Children

But God is not just King—He is Father. In Luke 15, Jesus tells the story of a son who dishonors his father, squanders his inheritance, and ends up living among pigs. Ashamed and broken, he returns home hoping just to be treated like a servant. But what does the father do?

> But while he was still a long way off, his father saw him and was filled with compassion for him; he ran to his son, threw his arms around him and kissed him.
>
> —Luke 15:20

No lecture. No punishment. Just embrace, restoration, and celebration. The son didn't have to prove his worth. He just had to come home.

And here's the beautiful truth: Children don't have to ask permission to belong. They don't have to wonder if they are allowed at the table. They don't need approval to open the refrigerator. They live in the house because it is their home. This is what it means to walk freely in relationship with God. You're not sneaking into the palace, hoping the guards don't stop you, or lingering in the hallway, hoping God has time for you. You're His child, and His door is always open.

So, Why Don't We Come?

There are several reasons we fail to approach God. Sometimes it's because of guilt, sometimes it's pride, and sometimes we forget how deeply loved we are. Freedom means that no matter what condition you're in, you can draw near.

- When you're full of faith or filled with fear
- When you've had a great week or a failing one
- When you know what to say and when all you have is a sigh

He still wants you and still welcomes you. You don't have to fix yourself to approach God. It's in His presence that healing begins.

This Is the Game Changer

Religion says, "Work your way to God." Grace says, "God made His way to you—now come freely." You have a permanent seat in the throne room. You have refrigerator rights in the Father's house. And you have a standing invitation to come boldly, not because of your goodness, but because of His grace.

Reflection Questions

1. Do you ever feel like you have to "clean yourself up" before coming to God? Why?

2. Which image from this chapter best helps you understand your relationship with God? Why?

3. What keeps you from approaching God freely?

4. How can you remind yourself that the throne room is open, even when you feel unworthy?

5. When you picture God listening to you pray, what emotions come up, and how does this chapter reshape that picture?

Notes

4

FREEDOM THROUGH THE SPIRIT

Now the Lord is the Spirit, and where the Spirit of the Lord is, there is freedom.
—2 Corinthians 3:17 (ESV)

There is a moment in every believer's life where the truth of freedom transitions from head knowledge to heart transformation. For some, that moment is instant. For others, it's gradual. But for all of us, it only happens through the power of the Holy Spirit.

The first three chapters of this book have laid a critical foundation, defining freedom in Christ, explaining how to break the grip of sin, and uncovering our direct access to God. But what makes these spiritual realities come alive? What transforms them from doctrine to daily experience? What gives us the power to walk freely? The answer is clear, and it's beautifully bold:

> "Where the Spirit of the Lord is, there is freedom."
>
> —2 Corinthians 3:17

Freedom is not self-willed. It's not the result of personality or performance. It's not a product of perfect theology. Freedom is the fruit of God's Spirit living in us.

The Missing Ingredient

Before Jesus ascended to heaven, He made a profound promise to His disciples:

> But you will receive power when the Holy Spirit comes on you; and you will be My witnesses…
>
> —Acts 1:8

This promise was a necessity. The disciples had spent three years walking with Jesus, hearing His words, watching Him perform miracles, and even participating in some themselves. But even after all of that, they were still afraid.

When Jesus was arrested, they scattered. Peter denied Him. Thomas doubted. They locked themselves in a room, uncertain, paralyzed by fear. And yet, just weeks later, they were standing in the public square, boldly preaching, healing the sick, and defying the religious authorities with unwavering courage. What changed? They didn't get a motivational speech. They didn't take leadership classes. They received the Holy Spirit.

> Then Peter, filled with the Holy Spirit, said to them…
>
> —Acts 4:8

> After they had prayed…they were all filled with the Holy Spirit and spoke the word of God boldly.
>
> —Acts 4:31

This was the turning point not only in their lives but also in the history of humanity. Pentecost was not just a decisive moment; it was the moment that birthed the Church and activated true, Spirit-filled freedom.

Dry Bones Don't Walk Freely

To understand the vital role of the Spirit, we can look to the Old Testament prophet Ezekiel. Ezekiel was a priest and prophet during Israel's Babylonian exile, a time when God's people were displaced, disheartened, and profoundly disconnected from God's promises. God used Ezekiel to deliver messages of both judgment and restoration, often through powerful and symbolic visions.

One of Ezekiel's most famous visions takes place in a valley of dry bones—a prophetic picture of a spiritually lifeless people (Ezekiel 37:1-14). God takes Ezekiel to this valley and asks, "Son of man, can these bones live?" Ezekiel wisely responds, "Sovereign Lord, You alone know."

Then God commands him to prophesy to the bones and to the breath (it's interesting to note that the Hebrew word used here for breath is *ruach*, and that is the same word for Spirit). As Ezekiel obeys, the bones begin to rattle and assemble. Tendons, flesh, and skin cover them. But they are still lying there lifeless until this moment in verse ten:

> So I prophesied as He commanded me, and breath entered them; they came to life and stood up on their feet—a vast army.
>
> —Ezekiel 37:10

This is more than a vision about Israel. It's a picture of us. Without the Spirit, we're present but powerless. We may have the structure of faith, the appearance of godliness, and even the desire to live, but only the breath of the Spirit gives true life and freedom.

Let's consider a few more biblical examples.

Jesus Modeled Spirit-Dependency

Though Jesus is fully God in the flesh, He chose to operate in complete dependence on the Holy Spirit. Before His public ministry began, He was baptized, and the Holy Spirit descended like a dove (Luke 3:21-22). Immediately after, He was "led by the Spirit into the wilderness" and overcame temptation (Luke 4:1-13). After that experience, Luke says:

> Jesus returned in the power of the Spirit…
>
> —Luke 4:14

Jesus was not only empowered by the Spirit—He was showing us how to live.

David's Plea and Saul's Loss

King David understood the importance of the Holy Spirit long before the day of Pentecost:

> Take not Your Holy Spirit from me.
>
> —Psalm 51:11

David had seen what happened to King Saul, a man who lost his way, grieved the Spirit, and descended into torment. When David sinned, he didn't just fear judgment; he feared losing the Spirit. He knew that without the Spirit, we're left with performance, fear, and control. With the Spirit, there is joy, renewal, and guidance.

Paul: From Chains to Champion

The author of 2 Corinthians 3:17 is no stranger to bondage or breakthrough. Paul once persecuted Christians, and he was bound by religious zeal and self-righteousness. But after encountering Jesus, he received the Holy Spirit, and everything changed.

He began preaching the gospel that he had once sought to destroy. He endured beatings, prison, and shipwrecks—all with unshakable freedom and authority. Why? Because, as he says in 2 Corinthians 3:17, "the Lord is the Spirit, and where the Spirit of the Lord is, there is freedom."

Paul didn't just teach theology. He lived it, empowered, emboldened, and filled with joy even in chains.

Spirit-Filled Freedom in Our Lives

You cannot walk freely without the Holy Spirit. You can believe in grace and still be bound. You can love Jesus and still feel powerless.

But when the Spirit comes—

- The fear that crippled you is replaced by peace.
- The sin that trapped you is broken by power.
- The shame that silenced you is shattered by truth.
- The confusion that clouded you is cleared by light.

The Holy Spirit does not just dwell in you to comfort—He empowers. Yes, He convicts, but He also counsels, strengthens, teaches, and leads. To walk freely is to walk in the Spirit.

> For all who are led by the Spirit of God are children of God.
> —Romans 8:14

The Locked Prison Door Revisited

Remember the prisoner from chapter one, sitting in a cell with the door wide open? Here's the full picture: The key to freely walking out isn't just the knowledge that the door is open. It's the grace to get up, take a step, and keep moving forward in freedom.

Many of us know we're forgiven. We know the door has been opened by Christ. Yet we stay seated, not because we want to remain stuck, but because we're tired. We've tried to change in our own strength. We've promised ourselves we'd do better, try harder, and not fall back again. Over time, that kind of effort wears us down.

Walking freely isn't about mental toughness or garnering stronger resolve. It's the daily choice to stop relying on ourselves and yield to the Holy Spirit. The Spirit doesn't shout commands from a distance. He comes alongside us to help us. The Spirit says:

- "You're free."
- "I'll walk with you."
- "You don't have to go back."

A Word to the Weary

If you've been trying to walk freely on your own, it makes sense that you're weary. Performance-based faith always leads to exhaustion. Legalism asks for constant effort but never gives lasting power. It promises control, but it leaves us frustrated and unfulfilled. This is not how the Christian life was meant to be lived.

This is your turning point. This is your Pentecost moment. Invite the Holy Spirit in, knowing He isn't waiting for you to be worthy. He's waiting for you to stop striving and simply ask Him to walk with you.

> "Not by might, nor by power, but by My Spirit," says the Lord Almighty.
>
> —Zechariah 4:6

Reflection Questions

1. Have you experienced the Holy Spirit personally? If so, how?

2. Why do you think many believers try to live free without depending on the Spirit?

3. Which of the above examples from Scripture resonates most with you (the disciples, Ezekiel, David, Paul), and why?

4. What does walking in the Spirit look like in your daily life?

5. Have you invited the Holy Spirit to fill and lead you? 'If not, what's stopping you?

Notes

5

FREEDOM IS A CHOICE

I will walk in freedom, for I have devoted myself to your commandments.
—Psalm 119:45 (NLT)

As we've just seen, the Spirit is the one who breaks our chains and breathes power into our walk. Without Him, we are helpless to live the life God calls us to. But with Him, we are not only free, but we are also empowered to choose. That's the beauty of grace: it doesn't remove our responsibility; it restores our ability.

Freedom is no longer a distant hope—it's a daily invitation. And now, with the Spirit living in us, we must decide how we'll walk. Because while Christ has made us free, walking in that freedom will always be a choice.

Freedom doesn't just happen to us. It's not something we drift into by accident or inherit by proximity to other believers. Freedom is a decision, a declaration, and a daily devotion. God offers us freedom, but does not force us to walk in it. From the very beginning, God has given humanity the dignity of choice.

The First Choice

Even in the Garden of Eden, when Adam and Eve had everything they needed, God placed a decision in front of them. He gave them freedom with boundaries, and He made it clear that love and obedience were meant to be chosen, not forced.

In the middle of this breathtaking garden stood the tree of the knowledge of good and evil (Genesis 2:9), and God told them plainly they were free to enjoy everything else, except that particular tree (Genesis 2:16-17). They could choose to obey and remain in communion with Him, trusting His goodness, or seek knowledge on their own terms and sever the relationship. Tragically, they chose to disobey.

In the aftermath, shame rushed in. Their eyes were opened, and suddenly they felt exposed. Instead of running to God, they started covering themselves and hiding (Genesis 3:7-8). They didn't just feel guilty about what they had done; their perception of themselves and God shifted (Genesis 2:25; 3:10-11). They hid themselves, separated not just by sin, but by the belief that they were no longer welcome.

Yet even then, God didn't just ask where they were; He came searching for them in the garden. He didn't come storming through the garden to destroy them. His posture was restoration.

Now, this is where the choice becomes subtler. It's easy to read that story and wonder, "What was so wrong with that tree anyway?" Or "Why would God withhold that if He's so good?" While these questions are very human, they point to the real tension beneath the surface. The temptation here wasn't just to eat the fruit, it was to decide whether God's wisdom could be trusted.

In that moment, Adam and Eve faced the same choice we still face today, which is to trust God's heart even when we don't understand the reasons, or to take control for ourselves. Sometimes choosing freedom means being willing to obey before we have all the answers. It means accepting that God's wisdom is higher than ours, even when our feelings suggest He's holding out.

Freedom to Choose Love

The same God who searched for Adam and Eve meets us now and still asks, "Where are you?" This is not because He doesn't know where we are, but because He wants us to know we still have a choice to come near.

At its core, choosing freedom involves recognizing how much we've been given and acknowledging God's goodness. The more we trust His heart, the more we understand that obedience isn't restriction, it's protection.

God didn't design us as robots. He gave us a will so that our love could be genuine, our surrender could be authentic, and our obedience could be meaningful. We cannot truly love God unless we have the freedom not to.

This is what makes freedom such a holy responsibility. When we surrender to God, we are not only choosing to walk away from sin, we are choosing to walk toward relationship, righteousness, and purpose. In other words, freedom isn't just the ability to say "no" to what destroys us. It's the ability to say "yes" to the One who loves us. But if we're honest, that choice isn't always easy. Sometimes we know exactly what God is asking, and we still hesitate, resist, or run the other way. That's why the story of Jonah is so powerful.

Jonah and the God Who Pursues

One of the clearest examples of this tension between God's sovereignty and human choice is found in the story of Jonah. God called Jonah to preach to the people of Nineveh, a wicked nation in desperate need of repentance. But Jonah refused. He ran in the opposite direction, boarding a ship to escape God's plan.

It might seem like Jonah didn't have a choice, but he did. God allowed Jonah to run. But in love, He pursued him. A storm arose, a fish swallowed him, and Jonah spent three days in darkness. Inside that fish, Jonah chose to pray. He decided to surrender. And when he did, God gave him a second chance.

Jonah's story teaches us that God's love is relentless, but our cooperation is also required. Jonah was not forced to obey, but God was committed to his destiny. Freedom means we can still say no, but grace means we're given another chance to say yes.

Safe Within God's Boundaries

We sometimes think of God's Word as limiting, but His commandments are not chains—they are guardrails that guide us. His precepts don't restrict our freedom, but instead, they protect it. Think of a playground surrounded by a fence. Within that space, children are free to run, explore, and play without fear of harm. The fence is a safeguard, not a prison. In the same way, the boundaries of God's Word allow us to live freely and safely in the life He has designed for us.

A Crossroad of Choice

In Mark 10, we see a blind man named Bartimaeus sitting by the roadside, reaching out for help. Over time, he figured out how to get by in his condition. People would recognize him by his blindness, which had become a part of who he was. When Bartimaeus heard Jesus was nearby, he passionately called out, "Jesus, Son of David, have mercy on me!" Even when others told him to stay silent, he kept shouting even louder. Deep inside, he felt that this moment was truly special and worth seizing (Mark 10:46-48).

After hearing him, Jesus paused for a moment and then asked a question that might seem a bit obvious: "What do you want Me to do for you?" (Mark 10:51). He wasn't confused about Bartimaeus's situation or trying to gather details; rather, He was offering a significant moment of decision.

Bartimaeus could have stayed where he was, hidden behind his circumstances and the expectations that had formed around him. Instead, he spoke it plainly: "Rabbi, I want to see." In that moment, Bartimaeus chose freedom. He chose to believe that life could be different. He chose to step out of the identity that had defined him for years and trust Jesus with what came next.

Jesus healed him, and Bartimaeus immediately started following Him on the road. That little detail really carries significance. Bartimaeus didn't just get his sight back; he was given a new purpose. When Jesus asked him a question, it wasn't only about healing. It was also about choosing to leave behind his old life and step into the new journey Jesus was inviting him to take.

Freedom often starts in a similar way for each of us. Jesus asks questions that encourage us to open up and respond. It's not because He's unaware of what we need, but because He genuinely wants us to make the choice, to name what's in our hearts, and to trust Him with it. Just like Bartimaeus, when we respond honestly, we discover that freedom isn't just something that's given to us; it's something we step into with faith and hope.

The freedom Christ offers is not just about release, it's about direction. You're not just set free *from* something. You're set free *for* something. And at every step, you must choose:

- Will I follow the flesh or the Spirit?
- Will I choose fear or faith?
- Will I live for myself or the Savior?

The world says, "Do what you want." Satan says, "Do what you will." But Jesus says, "Follow Me." Real freedom begins when we say, YES!

Reflection Questions

1. How does God's gift of free will affect the way you view your relationship with Him?

2. Have you ever, like Jonah, run from something God asked you to do? What happened?

3. In what areas of your life are you currently at a crossroads of choice?

4. How can God's commandments become a source of safety and peace rather than restriction?

5. What would it look like this week to intentionally choose the freedom God offers?

Notes

6

FREEDOM TO BE TRANSFORMED

And we all, who with unveiled faces contemplate the Lord's glory, are being transformed into His image with ever-increasing glory, which comes from the Lord, who is the Spirit.
—2 Corinthians 3:18

Freedom is not the finish line—it's the starting point of something far greater. When Christ sets us free, He doesn't just release us from bondage; He begins to reshape us from the inside out. The Bible calls this process transformation, and it's not something we manufacture. It's not the result of self-improvement, willpower, or religious routine. Real transformation happens by the power of the Holy Spirit.

> For this comes from the Lord who is the Spirit.
>
> —2 Corinthians 3:18 ESV

Just one verse after declaring that "where the Spirit of the Lord is, there is freedom," the apostle Paul shows us that freedom leads to metamorphosis, not just movement.

It's Not Just About Being Free, It's About Becoming Whole

You've been set free from sin. You've been invited to approach God boldly. You've received the Spirit of power and liberty. Now what?

Now comes the becoming.

God doesn't simply want you to be free from your past. He wants to reveal His image in you. Transformation is the unfolding of His character in your character, His mind in your mind, His grace in your responses. This is the Spirit's work.

A Better You or a New You?

The world offers endless strategies for self-transformation, including habit building, routines, mindset hacks, coaching, and therapy. Many of these tools can be helpful, but none of them can recreate your spirit. None of them can conform you to the image of Christ. Only the Spirit can do that.

When Paul speaks of transformation in 2 Corinthians 3, he uses a word that evokes profound, lasting change, not surface polish. The word "transformed" here is the Greek verb *metamorphoō*. It is the same word used for Jesus' transfiguration (Matthew 17:2). It speaks of becoming something altogether different, not just better, but new.

The Spirit Makes It Possible

Without the Holy Spirit, we may be able to change our behavior for a season, but we cannot change our nature. Only the Spirit can renew our minds, align our desires, and empower our walk. He doesn't just make you stronger. He makes you new.

- The Spirit brings conviction, as well as comfort and cleansing.
- He reveals the truth and then writes it on your heart.
- He shows you Jesus, and then shapes you to reflect Him.

This is why Paul said:

> So I say, walk by the Spirit, and you will not gratify the desires of the flesh.
>
> —Galatians 5:16

It's not by striving. It's by abiding in the Spirit who now lives within you.

The Butterfly Inside

Think of a caterpillar. It crawls on the ground, slow and limited, vulnerable and unseen. But a process is happening inside the cocoon, hidden from the world.

The butterfly is not a better version of the caterpillar. It's a new creation. It's not just a costume change. The same life that once crawled on the ground is transformed into something entirely new. This lowly creature that once crept along the leaves can rise into the air and see the world from a perspective the caterpillar could never imagine. So it is with you.

When the Spirit takes up residence in your life, He begins to work in hidden places. Sometimes it feels slow. Sometimes it's painful. But little by little, you are becoming someone brand new. And when the time is right, what has been changing on the inside will be revealed on the outside through your decisions, your peace, your love, your boldness.

Look at the Disciples—Again

We've already seen the disciples transformed after receiving the Holy Spirit at Pentecost. But notice that their change didn't stop with their bold expressions in public.

- Peter, who once acted rashly and fearfully, became a steady shepherd and father in the early Church (Matthew 16:22-23; Luke 22:54-62; John 21:15-17).
- John, who once wanted to call fire down from heaven, became known as the apostle of love (Luke 9:54-56; 1 John 4:7-12).
- Thomas, the doubter, became a bold witness, declaring Jesus as Lord, and standing faithfully with the disciples as the Church was born (John 20:24-29; Acts 1:13)

Their freedom in Christ, activated by the power of the Spirit, led to lasting transformation of character. And that same Spirit is working in you.

Zacchaeus: A Picture of Sudden Change

When Jesus came to the town of Jericho, a man named Zacchaeus climbed a tree to get a glimpse of Him. Zacchaeus was a greedy tax collector who was hated and known for exploiting his people. But everything changed in a single moment when Jesus saw him.

> …Zacchaeus, come down immediately. I must stay at your house today.
>
> —Luke 19:5

Jesus didn't give him a lecture. He gave him love. And Zacchaeus responded with radical transformation:

> But Zacchaeus stood up and said to the Lord, "Look, Lord! Here and now I give half of my possessions to the poor, and if I have cheated anybody out of anything, I will pay back four times the amount.
>
> —Luke 19:8

True transformation will always impact our habits, priorities, and attitude toward others. And when it's born of the Spirit, it doesn't take decades. It takes one surrendered encounter with Jesus. Zacchaeus didn't just get free. He got changed.

The Transformed Prisoner

Let's go back to that prisoner from chapter one. We've imagined what it meant for him to be free and unaware or aware but hesitant. Now imagine that same prisoner walking out, blinking in the sunlight. The chains are gone. He's finally breathing free air. But something inside him still feels bound. The memories, the labels, the shame still haunt him.

That's where the Holy Spirit comes in and whispers, "You're not who you were. You're not just out, you're new. You're clean. You're mine."

As the Spirit begins to heal and renew him, he starts to walk differently. He speaks differently. He doesn't just live like someone who was released; he lives like someone who was reborn.

That's transformation.

The Old Has Gone, the New Is Here

> Therefore, if anyone is in Christ, the new creation has come: The old has gone, the new is here!
>
> —2 Corinthians 5:17

The Holy Spirit doesn't just help us break free from the past. He writes a whole new future into our story. He's not patching you up, He's remaking you in the image of Christ. And the more time you spend with Him (in His Word, in prayer, in quiet surrender), the more you'll begin to notice the change. Not forced. Not fake. But fruitful.

> But the fruit of the Spirit is love, joy, peace, patience, kindness, goodness, faithfulness, gentleness, and self-control…
>
> —Galatians 5:22-23 (NKJV)

That's not the result of trying harder. That's the result of abiding.

You're Not Failing, You're Becoming

Maybe your transformation doesn't feel dramatic. Maybe you still struggle with things you thought would be gone by now. That doesn't mean you're failing. It means you're becoming.

Transformation is not about speed, it's about surrender. The Spirit knows how to grow you. Trust Him. Keep showing up. Keep saying yes. And day by day, step by step, you'll become more and more like Jesus.

Reflection Questions

1. Where do you see signs that God is transforming you, and where do you still feel stuck?

2. When facing change, do you rely more on your own effort or on the Holy Spirit? Why?

3. Which fruit of the Spirit do you most long to see grow in your life, and why?

4. What is one practical way you can cooperate with the Holy Spirit's work in you this week?

5. Where are you tempted to rush the process, and how can you trust God's timing instead?

Notes

7

FREEDOM TO SERVE OTHERS

You, my brothers and sisters, were called to be free. But do not use your freedom to indulge the flesh; rather, serve one another humbly in love.
—Galatians 5:13

In a world that often equates freedom with self-gratification, Scripture gives us a radical redefinition: freedom is the opportunity to serve. When God begins transforming us from the inside out, it doesn't end with personal renewal; it overflows into how we live, love, and serve.

True transformation always produces movement. The freedom we've received becomes the freedom we extend. And one of the most beautiful signs of a life being made new is a heart that begins to beat for others. In Christ, we are not only freed from sin, but we are also freed for service. Not as slaves of fear. Not as victims of obligation.

This is the paradox of the gospel. The more we understand what Jesus has done for us, the more we want to pour our lives out for others. Grace doesn't make us passive. Instead, it makes us generous. Love doesn't make us self-centered—it compels us to reach out to others.

True freedom doesn't say, "I'll do what I want."

It says, "I'm free to love as Christ did."

Jesus, the Servant King

No one modeled this freedom to serve more powerfully than Jesus. Though He was God, He took the form of a servant. He washed the feet of His disciples, including the one who would betray Him. He touched lepers, fed crowds, and dined with sinners. He made himself available to the broken and invisible.

Jesus's service was out of identity, not out of obligation. He served not to earn worth but to express it. He knew who He was, and because of that, He could kneel in service to others without shame. Walking in freedom means following His footsteps with confidence. We serve from a place of security, love, and abundance, not insecurity, fear, or lack.

Serving from Grace, Not Guilt

Sometimes we serve others not from joy, but from a deep sense of guilt, as if we're trying to make up for our mistakes or earn back God's favor. It may look like humility on the surface, but underneath is a quiet belief that we're not truly forgiven, so we should serve until we feel worthy again. But serving from penance is not freedom—it's another form of bondage.

One of the most powerful examples of this tension is found in the story of Peter. After boldly declaring that he would never deny Jesus, Peter failed, not once, but three times (Luke 22:33-34, 54-62). When the rooster crowed, the weight of what he had done hit him all at once. Shame crashed over him like a wave. He wept bitterly, disappearing into the background as Jesus was led to the cross. It's easy to imagine him wondering if he had disqualified himself forever. What could Jesus possibly do with someone like that?

Apparently…restore him.

After the resurrection, Jesus didn't avoid Peter or shame him. He went looking for him. Later, by the Sea of Galilee, Jesus spoke to Peter in a way that was both tender and unmistakably personal. In John 21:15-17 (NLT), Jesus asked him the same question three times, giving Peter a chance to return to love and purpose, not to fear and regret.

> "Simon son of John, do you love me…"
>
> "Yes, Lord," Peter replied, "you know I love you."
>
> "Then feed my sheep."

Instead of ignoring Peter's failure, Jesus met it with grace. He reaffirmed his calling and didn't disqualify him. Peter went on to become a bold leader in the early Church, not because he got everything right, but because he finally grasped the concept of grace.

God doesn't call the flawless—He calls the willing. And He doesn't want your service as a form of penance. He simply wants your life as a vessel. We don't serve others because we've failed. We serve others because He is faithful, His Spirit empowers us, and His love now flows through us.

When Service Becomes Striving

Many of us start out serving with joy and sincerity. But over time, if we're not careful, our motivations can shift.

- We serve out of obligation instead of love.
- We say yes to everything out of guilt or fear.
- We try to earn God's favor by doing more.
- We quietly believe that suffering in silence is a form of holiness.

This is legalism masquerading as obedience. It turns our acts of service into attempts at penance. It robs our joy and replaces intimacy with insecurity. And worst of all, it cuts us off from the very refreshing that Jesus offers.

The freedom Christ offers isn't permission to stop serving but a call to serve from a different place—one of grace, not guilt; love, not legalism; rest, not relentless striving. That kind of serving doesn't come from trying to pay God back; it stems from gratitude for what He's already done for us through Christ.

Gratitude as Motivation

We must never forget where we were when Jesus came for us. We were broken, bound, and blinded by sin. He lifted us, forgave us, filled us with His Spirit, and gave us new life. That memory should never become dull and should stir us to action.

When we truly grasp how much Christ has done for us, gratitude will overflow. We will begin to see people not as burdens but as opportunities. Our service becomes a thank-you note written with our lives.

The Bible outlines three powerful traits of Christlike service:

1. **Serve Humbly (No Personal Agenda)**
   We don't serve to be seen. We serve because we've seen Christ.

   > Beware of practicing your righteousness before other people in order to be seen by them…when you give to the needy, do not let your left hand know what your right hand is doing…And your Father who sees in secret will reward you.
   >
   > —Matthew 6:1-4 (ESV)

2. **Give Freely (Uninhibited and Graciously)**
   True generosity is not measured by the amount we give, but by the heart behind it.

   > God loves a cheerful giver…you will always have plenty… so that you can give to every good work.
   >
   > —2 Corinthians 9:7-9 (paraphrased)

3. **Trust That God Will Reward You**
   When we pour ourselves out, God pours back in.

   > Giving help to the poor is like loaning money to the Lord. He will pay you back for your kindness.
   >
   > —Proverbs 19:17 (ERV)

We Are the Extension of Grace

When we serve others, we become the hands and feet of Christ. Our time, our talent, and our treasures become tools in the hands of a loving God. Someone's breakthrough may come through your obedience. Someone's healing may flow through your compassion. Your generosity may ignite someone's salvation.

Freedom gives us the ability to step outside ourselves and enter into the needs of others, carrying hope, healing, and hospitality everywhere we go.

Reflection Questions

1. How does the world's definition of freedom differ from the Bible's?

2. In what ways has gratitude for what Jesus has done stirred you to serve others?

3. Are there areas in your life where you've withheld your gifts, time, or resources out of fear or self-preservation?

4. Who around you might be waiting for an expression of Christ's love through your service?

5. What's one step you can take this week to serve someone in humility and joy?

Notes

8

FREEDOM TO BE REFRESHED

A generous person will prosper; whoever
refreshes others will be refreshed.
—Proverbs 11:25

Serving others is a sacred privilege, but even the most willing hearts can grow weary. When we give and pour out, it's easy to forget that we're the vessel, not the source. Freedom in Christ not only invites us to serve but also invites us to stop and be renewed.

True freedom permits us to rest, to be replenished, and to drink deeply from the well of God's presence. This next step on our journey reminds us that rest is not a sign of weakness, but a sign of worship.

The Christian life is not meant to be one of constant depletion. Yet far too often, that's exactly how we live. We run on empty, drained by the demands of life, ministry, family, and service. We give, we pour, we sacrifice, and then wonder why we feel burned out, bitter, or buried beneath exhaustion.

But that was never God's intention. In Christ, we have the freedom not just to work but to be refreshed. Not just to serve but to thrive. Not just to pour out but to be filled again and again.

The Savior Syndrome

Sometimes what robs us of refreshment isn't the intensity of life—it's the illusion that we're responsible for everyone in it. Without realizing it, we slip into a subtle form of self-righteousness that leads us to attempt to fix, rescue, or carry others in ways that only God can.

We become their emotional safety net, their spiritual compass, and their primary source of strength, but in doing so, we exhaust ourselves and often get in the way of what God is trying to do in their lives. There is a fine line between compassion and control. Our love serves, but it does not save. Only Jesus saves.

When we feel driven to always be the answer, we rob others of their opportunity to seek the Answer. And we rob ourselves of the stillness we desperately need to hear from God for our own souls. Even Jesus—the actual Savior—would often withdraw from the crowds. He didn't meet every need or respond to every request. He knew the importance of boundaries because His strength flowed from intimacy with the Father, not from the demands of people.

You are not the vine. You are a branch. Your job is not to supply the life; it's to stay connected to the One who does.

The Refreshing from the Lord

When we stop striving to be everything for everyone and let go of the pressure to save, fix, or carry what only God can handle, we create space for refreshing from the Lord, which is far more powerful than anything we can do in our own strength.

This kind of rest isn't found in a vacation or a nap. It's a supernatural renewal of the soul that flows from God's presence through the Holy Spirit.

We see this beautifully depicted in Acts 3. Peter and John encounter a man who had been lame from birth and carried daily to the temple gate to beg. His life was marked by dependence and limitation. He wasn't expecting healing—he was simply hoping for enough to get through the day. But instead of giving the man what he expected, Peter offered what only Jesus could provide:

> In the name of Jesus Christ of Nazareth, walk.
>
> —Acts 3:6b

And with that declaration, the man was miraculously healed. His legs were strengthened, his hope restored. He didn't just walk, but he jumped and praised God in the very place he had once begged.

This moment became a powerful picture of what it looks like to be revived by God's presence. It wasn't about effort. It wasn't about striving. It was about receiving.

As a crowd gathered in awe, Peter used the opportunity to speak a more profound truth:

> Repent therefore, and turn back, that your sins may be blotted out, that times of refreshing may come from the presence of the Lord…
>
> —Acts 3:19, ESV

Peter connected the man's physical restoration to the greater invitation for spiritual renewal. Just like the man at the gate, we don't earn refreshing by doing more, but we receive it by returning to the One who restores. Repentance, in this context, isn't just about shame or contrition. It's about reorientation, which involves turning back toward the presence of God.

The Holy Spirit revives what life has depleted. He breathes life into dry bones. He brings clarity to weary minds and joy to burdened hearts. This is the cycle of spiritual refreshing:

- We release.
- We return.
- We receive.

This refreshing is a gift for the surrendered, and not a reward for perfection. And it's one we need daily. Freedom means we no longer have to power through life on fumes. We don't need to prove our worth or earn our rest. Instead, we sit at the feet of the One who is everything, and from that place of intimacy, we are refreshed, not just emotionally, but spiritually. Not just temporarily, but eternally.

This is the gift of grace: to release what was never ours to carry, and to receive what we could never earn, including rest, renewal, and the restoring breath of God.

The Cycle of Refreshing

Proverbs 11:25 presents a divine paradox. When we refresh others, we are refreshed in return. But how? Isn't giving supposed to drain us?

It's true that serving can deplete us. Even Jesus grew physically tired and withdrew to pray (Luke 5:15). The difference is that being depleted from loving people well is not the same as being drained from serving without God's strength. Depletion is often a signal that we've poured out faithfully, and now we need to be replenished. Drained is often a warning that we've been carrying what God never asked us to carry.

When serving is done in the Spirit, flowing from intimacy with Christ, it does not drain us. When we offer what He has already multiplied in us, He refreshes us in return. This is the cycle of refreshing God has designed:

1. We receive from God.
2. We pour out what we've received.
3. God replenishes us with more.
4. The process continues, deeper and richer each time.

But when we try to serve without first receiving, we disrupt that cycle. We become like a hose disconnected from the Source, still trying to water others but running dry.

The Feeding of the 5,000

There's a moment in John 6 that gives us a beautiful picture of what refreshing looks like in the hands of Jesus. A massive crowd of 5,000 men, not including women and children, had gathered to hear Him. They were tired, hungry, and needy. The disciples saw the need and panicked. Jesus turned to Philip and asked a question:

> Where shall we buy bread for these people to eat?
>
> —John 6:5

It was a test, not because Jesus didn't know the answer, but because He already knew what He was going to do (John 6:6). He wanted Philip to zoom out to trust the Provider more than the problem. The disciples found a boy who offered them his five barley loaves and two fish. The meal was hardly enough for a family, let alone thousands. And yet, Jesus took what was offered, gave thanks, broke it, and multiplied it until everyone was fed, with twelve baskets left over.

Don't miss this:

- Jesus involved the disciples in the miracle.
- He had them instruct the people to sit down on the green grass (Mark 6:39), which is a visual echo of Psalm 23, which says, "He makes me lie down in green pastures."
- He asked them to distribute what He had already blessed and broken.
- He fed the multitudes, but the disciples still carried the miracle to the people.

This is the rhythm of refreshing.

We bring what little we have. Jesus receives it, blesses it, and returns it multiplied. Then we carry it to others, not out of pressure, but out of partnership.

And in that process, we are fed.

Rest Is Not a Reward, It's a Rhythm

Some of us believe rest must be earned. We'll rest once we've finished the list, completed the task, and resolved the crisis. But in God's design, rest is not a reward. It's a rhythm built into creation, modeled in Christ, and offered as a gift.

When we walk in freedom, we permit ourselves to pause, breathe, and be human. We say no without guilt. We step away without shame. We find time in the presence of God to be filled again. Because when we're refreshed, we can refresh others with joy, not resentment; with power, not burnout.

Reflection Questions

1. Do you feel more depleted or drained right now, and what do you think God is inviting you to do in response?

2. What might it look like for you to reenter the cycle of refreshing that includes receiving, giving, and being refilled?

3. How does the story of Jesus feeding the 5,000 shift your perspective on offering what little you have?

4. Where do you think God is inviting you to rest now, physically, emotionally, or spiritually?

5. Are there areas of your life where you need to reconnect to the Source before you pour out again?

Notes

9

FREEDOM FROM THE OPINIONS OF OTHERS

Am I now trying to win the approval of human beings or of God? Or am I trying to please people? If I were still trying to please people, I would not be a servant of Christ.
—Galatians 1:10

One of the most crippling prisons we can live in is the one built from the opinions of others. It's subtle at first, seeking approval, validation, and applause. However, our joy is soon contingent on someone else's reaction. Our confidence rises and falls with their approval. We filter our calling through their expectations. We shrink back from purpose because of their disapproval. This isn't freedom. It's bondage in disguise.

The gospel offers us a better way: the freedom to live for an audience of one. GOD.

Living for the Audience of One

To really appreciate why Paul's words in Galatians 1:10 are so powerful, it's helpful to peek behind the scenes. The believers in Galatia had begun their faith journey, embracing the message of Jesus and the incredible grace of God. They were discovering that salvation is a wonderful gift, not something we can earn.

But not long after, some other teachers showed up, encouraging them to follow extra religious rules to be truly accepted. They gave the impression that faith in Jesus alone wasn't enough. They also cast doubt on Paul's authority and intentions, implying he was preaching grace just because it was popular and easier to listen to.

That's why Paul's response is so direct. He isn't trying to win a debate or protect his reputation. He's fighting for their freedom. He knows that the moment you start adjusting the truth to keep people happy, you slowly trade your peace for pressure, and your calling for approval.

Paul was writing to believers in Galatia who were being swayed by legalistic teachers. These influencers questioned Paul's authority, saying he wasn't strict enough, wasn't traditional enough, and that his message of grace was too good to be true.

Rather than change his message to win them over, Paul drew a line in the sand. He made it clear that you can't live for people's approval and serve Christ at the same time. You will either shape your life to be accepted by men or surrender it to follow God.

This is a tension we all feel. We have a need to be liked and often fear rejection. This leads to the quiet pressure to water down the truth or play it safe so we don't ruffle feathers. But Paul reminds us that the moment we base our message, our obedience, or our worth on public opinion, we're no longer walking in the freedom Christ offers.

To live freely, we must live for the Audience of One.

Paul could endure beatings, imprisonment, and mockery because his identity was rooted not in applause, but in assignment. He knew who had called him. He knew whose voice mattered most. And so must we.

From Saul of Tarsus to Apostle Paul

Let's take a closer look at the story of Saul of Tarsus, later known as the Apostle Paul.

Saul's story is one of the most explicit pictures in Scripture of what it looks like to break free from living for people's approval and learn to live for God's voice instead. His transformation into the Apostle Paul is told in the book of Acts, including the moment Jesus meets him on the road to Damascus and everything that follows (Acts 9; see also Acts 22 and Acts 26). It's such a powerful reminder that when Jesus becomes the One you're living for, the opinions around you don't get to have the final say.

Before encountering Jesus, Saul was driven by a desire for public approval and a quest for religious status. He had pedigree, knowledge, and the respect of Jewish leaders. He was zealous to the point of persecuting Christians in defense of tradition. Saul was everything the religious system applauded.

Then, he met Jesus on the road to Damascus.

That encounter left him blind, but it also left him changed. When his sight was restored, so was his identity. He was no longer Saul, the persecutor, but Paul, the apostle. He traded reputation for revelation. He went from a feared enforcer to a fearless evangelist.

But let's not forget that Paul still had to wrestle with the perceptions of others. The early Christians didn't trust him. The Jewish leaders now hated him. The very people whose approval he once craved now saw him as a traitor. Paul had to walk in obedience to God even when others doubted his transformation. And yet, he kept going.

He planted churches. He wrote letters. He endured beatings, imprisonments, and rejection. And through it all, he made it clear that he was living for God's approval rather than human applause.

Today, we cherish the Scriptures he wrote. But they were born from a man who chose God's purpose over people's praise.

Who Do You Say I Am?

Long before Paul ever challenged the Church to live for God's approval instead of man's, Jesus Himself modeled this with quiet strength. The crowd never swayed him, but He was fully aware of what they thought.

Matthew 16:13 is a moment in Scripture that reveals just how intentional He was about separating public opinion from divine identity.

> When Jesus came to the region of Caesarea Philippi, he asked his disciples, "Who do people say the Son of Man is?"
>
> —Matthew 16:13

To fully grasp the weight of Jesus' question, we must understand where He was when He asked it and why that matters. Jesus and His disciples had traveled to the region of Caesarea Philippi, a Roman-influenced city known for its idolatry and pagan worship. Statues of gods lined the public places, and shrines were built into the cliffs to honor false deities, such as Pan and Caesar himself. This wasn't just a scenic stop—it was a spiritually charged atmosphere, full of competing claims to divinity and cultural pressure to conform.

It's there, in a place saturated with noise, opinion, and false worship, that Jesus asked His disciples who people said He was. They responded with a list of public theories:

> Some say John the Baptist, others say Elijah, and still others, Jeremiah or one of the prophets.
>
> —Matthew 16:14

The crowd had plenty to say about Jesus. Some of it was flattering, some of it was wild, none of it was accurate. Then Jesus asked the more important question:

> "Who do you say I am?" Simon Peter answered, "You are the Messiah, the Son of the living God."
>
> —Matthew 16:14

And Jesus responded with affirmation, saying that Peter's insight didn't come from popular opinion or human reasoning, but from a revelation from the Father.

This moment teaches us a vital lesson: truth is not determined by consensus, and identity is not anchored in public opinion. Not even Jesus, the sinless Son of God, was correctly identified by the crowd. So why are we surprised when we're misunderstood, mislabeled, or misjudged? Freedom comes when we stop basing our worth on what others say and start living by what God has revealed to us through Christ.

Our Identity Is in Christ

When we root our identity in people's opinions, we live like spiritual orphans who are always striving, never settled. But when we root our identity in Christ, we become unshakable. Our worth is not based on someone else's affirmation but on God's declaration.

> This is my Son, whom I love; with him I am well pleased.
> —Matthew 3:17

That's what the Father spoke over Jesus before He did a single miracle. That's the identity we receive, too, not because of what we do, but because of who we are.

Living Unapologetically Free

To walk freely means we no longer allow the fear of man to silence our voice or steer our decisions.

- We can love people without being ruled by their opinions.
- We can honor others without compromising our call.
- We can walk in grace, even when misunderstood.

The opinions of others will always fluctuate. But God's opinion of you is rooted in truth, anchored in grace, and unchanging in love. Let's walk in the freedom that comes from knowing who we are and whose we are.

Reflection Questions

1. Whose opinion has had the most significant impact on your identity or choices in the past?

2. How does Paul's transformation encourage you in your journey of boldness and freedom?

3. Are there areas in your life where you're still seeking approval from others more than from God?

4. What would it look like for you to walk in the confidence of God's opinion of you today?

5. How can rooting your identity in Christ help you navigate criticism, rejection, or misunderstanding?

Notes

10

FREEDOM TO LOVE WITHOUT FEAR

There is no fear in love.
But perfect love drives out fear.
—1 John 4:18a

Love is risky. It exposes us to rejection, vulnerability, and disappointment. But love is also one of the clearest signs of God's work in us and one of the most powerful expressions of freedom.

When we're bound by fear, we protect ourselves from people. We build walls. We guard our hearts not in wisdom but in self-preservation. But when God's love frees us, we begin to love others without fear of being hurt, misunderstood, or taken for granted because our love isn't sourced in others, it's anchored in Christ.

Fearless Love and the Alabaster Jar

Even in Jesus' time, loving openly came at a cost. This was especially true for the broken, the outcast, or the misunderstood. One of the most powerful examples of fearless love is found in Luke 7:36-50, where a woman with a sinful reputation did something scandalous—and sacred.

Jesus had been invited to dine at the home of a Pharisee named Simon. As they sat at the table, a woman from the city entered, known by her reputation, though never named. She brought an alabaster jar of expensive perfume, and as she stood behind Jesus, weeping, she began to wash His feet with her tears, dry them with her hair, kiss them, and pour out the perfume upon them.

This was a social disruption and an act of profound vulnerability. She had no guarantee of being received. She was not invited. She risked judgment, rejection, and even humiliation. But she came anyway.

Why? Because she had encountered perfect love, and it set her free. She knew what Jesus had done for her, and the forgiveness He offered had unlocked something in her soul that fear could no longer hold back. She didn't care about the whispers. She wasn't bound by reputation. She didn't flinch at the glares. Her love was pure and unrestrained. This was not because she was shameless, but because she had been set free from shame.

The Significance of the Alabaster Jar

Alabaster jars were designed to hold precious oils and perfumes. They were costly and sealed, so breaking one was a one-time act—a total outpouring, not a measured dose. The contents were often worth a year's wages, and they were reserved for burial or special honor.

In offering this perfume, she was giving something valuable and also pouring out her past, her gratitude, and her heart in worship. It was an offering of reckless, fearless love. Jesus didn't rebuke her. He honored her. He told the Pharisee, "She loved much, because she was forgiven much."

Real Love Is Not Insecure

Many of us fear loving fully because we fear rejection, betrayal, or inadequacy. We've been hurt before, and loving again feels like a risk. But the freedom Christ gives roots us in His perfect love, which drives out fear (1 John 4:18).

Sometimes the fear isn't of punishment—it's fear of exposure. It's the fear of being fully known and not fully loved. It's the fear of offering your heart and watching someone mishandle it. We fear vulnerability because we associate it with loss. However, in the kingdom of God, vulnerability is the soil in which love grows.

But the truth is, Christlike love doesn't begin with what others do to us. Instead, it flows from what Christ has done in us. We don't love to be loved back. We love because we are already secure.

When we are anchored in His acceptance, we are no longer at the mercy of other people's responses. Love becomes a gift, not a gamble. We can pour ourselves out like the woman with the alabaster jar, not because people are safe, but because God is our refuge.

This is what it means to walk freely:

- To love boldly, not cautiously.
- To risk kindness when bitterness feels safer.
- To forgive when it's not requested.
- To pour out when we may not be poured into.

Not because we are fearless by nature, but because His love has secured us.

Jesus loved us while we were still sinners. He poured Himself out when we had nothing to offer in return. And now He invites us to do the same, not under pressure, but in freedom.

Peter's Restoration

There may be no better example of freedom to love again than the story of Peter, the bold disciple who denied Jesus at His most critical moment.

When Jesus was arrested, Peter followed at a distance. But when pressed about his association with Jesus, he denied it, not once, but three times. Earlier that night, Peter was full of zeal. He told Jesus he would never fall away, that he was willing to go to prison, even willing to die with Him (Luke 22:33). But Jesus gently told him the truth, not to shame him, but to prepare him. He said Peter would deny even knowing Him three times before the rooster crowed (Luke 22:34).

And after the rooster crowed, Peter locked eyes with Jesus and ran away, weeping bitterly. Shame consumed him. But the story didn't end there.

After the resurrection, Jesus appeared to Peter again—this time not with judgment but with restoration. On the shore of Galilee, Jesus asked Peter three times, "Do you love Me?" Each time, Peter answered yes. Each time, Jesus responded: "Feed my sheep."

Jesus didn't just forgive Peter. He recommissioned him, and He affirmed Peter's purpose. He invited him back into fellowship and entrusted him with caring for others. That's the power of love. That's the freedom Jesus offers.

When we know we're loved by God—even after our worst failure—we are free to love others, too.

Love That's Rooted in Grace

The kind of love God calls us to isn't earned, conditional, or based on performance. It's grace-based. It's the kind of love that Jesus extended to Zacchaeus, to Peter, to the woman with the alabaster box, and to you and me. This love:

- Covers a multitude of sins (1 Peter 4:8)
- Binds us together in unity (Colossians 3:14)
- Is patient, kind, and never fails (1 Corinthians 13)

When we walk in this love, we walk freely. We're not worried about measuring up. We're not ruled by resentment. We're not consumed by self-interest. We give. We serve. We forgive. We embrace.

And we do it fearlessly because perfect love casts out fear.

A Life Marked by Love

Freedom is not a license to live for ourselves. Freedom is the power to live like Christ. Jesus loved radically. He touched the untouchable. He welcomed the outcast. He washed feet. He laid down His life.

When we love others, we're most like Jesus. This is not a soft sentiment. It's not a feel-good emotion. It's costly. It's courageous. And it's liberating. You are free to love. Not because it's safe, but because you're secure in Christ.

Reflection Questions

1. Where are you holding back love out of fear? What would change if you believed God's love is truly perfect?

2. How does Peter's restoration encourage you in your own journey of failure and redemption?

3. What would it look like for you to love someone without expecting anything in return?

4. In what relationships is God inviting you to love more boldly or forgive more freely?

5. How can embracing God's love for you help you love others from a place of freedom?

Notes

11

FREEDOM TO FORGIVE YOURSELF

If we confess our sins, he is faithful and just and will forgive us our sins and purify us from all unrighteousness.
—1 John 1:9

Sometimes, the hardest person to forgive is yourself. We may believe that God has forgiven us. We may even know others have moved on. But we replay the failures, relive the shame, and rehearse the regret. We feel unworthy of grace and disqualified from purpose.

But freedom in Christ includes freedom to forgive yourself, because to withhold forgiveness from yourself is to act as if your standard is higher than God's.

What Are You Still Carrying?

Think of the weight some of us carry every day. A broken past. A moral failure. A missed opportunity. A harsh word we can't take back. A decision we wish we could undo. That weight becomes a burden we were never meant to bear. And in response, Jesus says:

> Come to Me, all who are weary and burdened, and I will give you rest.
>
> —Matthew 11:28

You are not meant to carry your past like a badge of shame. You are intended to lay it down and receive rest, healing, and renewal. When we cling to guilt, we're essentially saying the cross wasn't enough, when the cross was more than enough. The blood of Jesus covers everything, not just the things we think are forgivable.

When God Moves On, So Should You

It's one thing to believe that God forgives us. It's another to live as if it were true. Many of us carry guilt for what we've done or shame for what was done to us long after God has already released us. We struggle with memories, regret, and the quiet question, "How could God still use someone like me?" But throughout Scripture, we see men who had to make the same choice to walk forward, not because they felt worthy, but because God's mercy was greater than their past, and his calling on their lives was still very real. Let's look at two lives that model what it means to forgive yourself and live freely in God's calling, even after moral failure and deep regret.

David: The King Who Knew Guilt and Grace

David is often remembered for his boldness against Goliath and his heartfelt psalms. But one of his darkest moments is rarely emphasized. It came after he misused his power as king to commit adultery with Bathsheba, the wife of Uriah, and then plotted Uriah's death to cover it up (2 Samuel 11). It was a deliberate, layered sin. It was not simply a moment of weakness, but a series of choices that cost lives and broke trust.

When the prophet Nathan confronted him, David didn't make excuses. He confessed: "I have sinned against the Lord" (2 Samuel 12:13). He wept, fasted, and poured out his sorrow in what became Psalm 51, crying:

> "Wash me thoroughly from my iniquity…"
>
> "Against You, You only, have I sinned…"
>
> "Create in me a clean heart, O God…"
>
> "Restore to me the joy of Your salvation…"
>
> —Psalm 51:1-12 (NKJV)

David's sin had consequences, but he didn't let guilt define his future. That's the turning point for all of us. God's forgiveness is real, but we still have to decide whether we'll keep punishing ourselves after He's already shown us mercy. In fact, Scripture says there came a moment when David got up from the ground, washed, changed his clothes, and returned to worship (2 Samuel 12:20). He didn't pretend it never happened, but he refused to stay buried under it. God still called him "a man after My own heart."

David didn't move on quickly, but he did move forward. Forgiving yourself doesn't mean pretending it never happened; it means believing that grace is stronger than your failure.

Moses: The Fugitive with a Calling

Before Moses led Israel out of Egypt, he was a man with blood on his hands. In Exodus 2, he saw an Egyptian abusing a Hebrew slave. In a moment of rage, he struck the man down and buried the body. After word got out, Moses fled Egypt and spent the next 40 years in the wilderness—tending sheep, far from his people and possibly from peace. And that's what guilt and shame often do. They don't just make us regret what happened. They convince us to hide, withdraw, and settle into a life that feels safer than facing the future.

When God called him through the burning bush (Exodus 3), Moses pushed back:

> "Who am I?"
>
> "What if they don't believe me?"
>
> "I am slow of speech."

This wasn't just a list of insecurities. They were words of self-condemnation. Moses believed his past disqualified him from the future God was offering. In other words, God was calling him forward, but Moses was still punishing himself. But God disagreed with Moses's assessment. "I will be with you," He said. And that was enough.

Moses returned. He faced Pharaoh. He led his people through miracles, deserts, and waters, not as a perfect man, but as a forgiven, called, and obedient one.

Moses shows us that God can call us out of the wilderness, not just physically but emotionally as well. Your shame doesn't have the final say; God's calling does. Forgiving yourself is often the crucial step that helps you stop living in hiding and start walking in freedom again.

The Prisoner Who Forgot He Was Free

Remember the man we imagined sitting in a prison cell, long after his pardon had been signed? The door is open. The release papers are official. But he's still seated on a cold bench, head down, chained not by iron but by invisible guilt. That's what it feels like when we don't forgive ourselves.

God has declared us free through the cross, the resurrection, and the blood of Jesus. He no longer holds our sins against us. But sometimes, we hold them against ourselves, rehearsing shame He's already removed.

Self-forgiveness is the moment we decide to stand up, walk out, and live like the prison gate is genuinely open. The voice of shame says, "You don't deserve to move forward." The voice of God says, "You are already free. Now walk in it." You are not the sum of your failures. You are the evidence of God's mercy.

God's Forgiveness Is Final

There's no footnote to God's forgiveness. No conditions. There is no second-tier grace. When He forgives, it's complete.

> As far as the east is from the west, so far has he removed our transgressions from us.
>
> —Psalm 103:12

If God has removed it, why are you still carrying it? If God has forgotten it, why are you still remembering it? If God has called you clean, why are you calling yourself condemned? Freedom to forgive yourself means agreeing with God. It means aligning your internal narrative with His eternal truth.

Shame and the Garden

Let's revisit Adam and Eve in the garden. After they sinned, they hid from God. But it wasn't just guilt that drove them into the bushes; it was shame. Guilt says, "I did something wrong." Shame says, "I am something wrong."

And shame separates us, not just from God, but from ourselves. It makes us forget who we really are in Christ. Instead of seeing ourselves through God's eyes, we start seeing ourselves only through our worst moments. Shame convinces us that failure is our identity, preventing us from living as someone God has already redeemed.

What was God's posture toward Adam and Eve after they had sinned? He came looking for them (Genesis 3:8-9). He asked questions not to condemn but to restore (Genesis 3:9-13). He made a covering for them, clothing them when they could not cover themselves (Genesis 3:21). He didn't ignore their sin, but He didn't abandon them either. That same love meets us today.

Jesus took our shame on the cross. He bore it, so we don't have to. He wore the weight of our guilt so we could wear the robe of righteousness. We're not just forgiven—we're made new.

The Path Forward

Forgiving yourself is not about minimizing what happened. It's about accepting it and magnifying what Jesus has done. It's not denial; it's deliverance. It's not pretending it never happened. It's proclaiming that your past no longer defines your future.

Reflection Questions

1. What failure or regret are you still carrying that God has already forgiven?

2. Why do you think it's often harder to forgive yourself than to accept God's forgiveness?

3. How do the stories of Adam and Eve, Moses, and David highlight God's grace even in the midst of shame?

4. Based on the examples in this chapter, how can you encourage yourself when self-condemnation arises?

5. What would your life look like if you lived fully in the freedom of God's forgiveness?

Notes

12

FREEDOM TO PERSEVERE

Let us not become weary in doing good, for at the proper time we will reap a harvest if we do not give up.
—Galatians 6:9

Freedom doesn't mean we won't face difficulties. It doesn't mean we'll never want to quit. But it does mean we have access to a strength greater than our own—a grace that empowers us to persevere.

To persevere is to continue moving forward despite feeling like giving up. It's continuing to believe when everything in you wants to doubt. It's staying faithful when the fruit isn't visible, the path isn't easy, and the reward seems far off. God doesn't just free us from things. Instead, He frees us for endurance and equips us for the long road.

The Story of Joseph—From Prisoner to Prince

Joseph's life is a clear biblical example of perseverance in the face of injustice. As a young man, Joseph received dreams from God about his future. These dreams foretold his rise to leadership and influence, but his life seemed to spiral in the opposite direction.

His brothers, driven by jealousy, sold him into slavery. He was taken far from home, stripped of his identity, and falsely accused. He was thrown into prison, forgotten, misunderstood, and left waiting for justice. But Joseph didn't quit.

Through every setback, he persevered with integrity. He interpreted dreams in prison. He honored God when no one was watching. He kept showing up, trusting that the God who gave him the dream would also fulfill it. And in time, God did.

Joseph was elevated to the second-highest position in Egypt, and he became a rescuer to his people. He forgave his brothers. And he saw the hand of God not only in his blessing, but in his brokenness.

> You intended to harm me, but God intended it for good to accomplish what is now being done, the saving of many lives.
>
> —Genesis 50:20

Joseph's story reminds us that God is still at work, even in the waiting.

The Freedom Found in Perseverance

Walking in freedom doesn't mean walking on clouds. Sometimes it means walking through fire and trusting that God is still with you even when you can't feel Him. Perseverance is not the absence of struggle; it's the refusal to let struggle define you. It's a mindset of freedom that declares, "I belong to God, and I will not be moved."

There's a unique kind of liberty that only emerges when you've had to stand through suffering. It's the kind of freedom that doesn't wait for everything to make sense before it believes. It's the confidence that even in the valley, God is still good and still worthy of trust.

This is the kind of freedom Job, Hannah, and the three Hebrew boys lived out. Their stories remind us that God's silence is not His absence, His delays are not His denials, and His presence is not proven by ease, but often revealed in the fire. Each of them chose to trust, not because of what they saw, but because of who they knew God to be. That's the kind of freedom that perseveres.

Job, the Man Who Refused to Curse God

Job was a man of integrity. He was wealthy, respected, and righteous before God. But in a sudden and unthinkable sequence, Job lost everything, including his children, his wealth, and his health. His body was covered in sores, his friends turned against him, and his wife told him to give up: "Curse God and die" (Job 2:9). But Job didn't.

Instead, he tore his robe, fell to the ground, and worshiped. He said:

> The Lord gave and the Lord has taken away; blessed be the name of the Lord.
>
> —Job 1:21

In the chapters that follow, Job pours out raw lament. He questions, he weeps, and he argues with God, but he never lets go of his reverence or belief. And at the height of his agony, he utters one of the most powerful declarations of perseverance in all of Scripture:

> Though He slay me, yet will I hope in Him.
>
> —Job 13:15

In the end, God speaks to Job, not with easy answers, but with divine perspective. He restores him, blesses him again, and vindicates his integrity. But the true miracle was not what Job regained. The miracle was that he never lost his faith.

Job shows us that perseverance doesn't mean smiling through suffering—it means worshiping anyway. It means choosing trust when you have every reason not to.

Hannah, the Woman Who Prayed Through the Pain

Hannah's heart ached for a child. Year after year, she watched others celebrate motherhood while she endured infertility and ridicule. She was taunted. Her own husband didn't understand her grief. And even the priest mistook her deep sorrow for drunkenness (1 Samuel 1).

But Hannah didn't shut down. She didn't lash out. She didn't give up. She kept coming to the temple. She kept praying. She poured out her soul before the Lord without attempts at polished words, but with anguish and honesty.

Eventually, God heard her cry and gave her a son, Samuel, who would become one of the greatest prophets in Israel's history. But Hannah's breakthrough didn't come because she earned it. It came because she refused to let bitterness or delay rob her of intimacy with God.

> In bitterness of soul Hannah wept much and prayed to the Lord… I was pouring out my soul to the Lord.
>
> —1 Samuel 1:10,15

Hannah teaches us that prayer is perseverance in its purest form. Sometimes freedom isn't loud or visible. Instead, it's the quiet decision to show up again, trust again, and believe that God sees you.

Perseverance Is the Posture of Freedom

In a culture obsessed with instant results and painless victories, God calls us to a deeper freedom that perseveres. It's the kind of freedom that says:

"Even if I don't see the promise yet, I will not quit."

"Even if the healing hasn't come, I will still praise."

"Even if I don't understand the why, I will trust the Who."

This kind of freedom is only possible when we anchor ourselves to the character of God, not our circumstances. We don't endure because we're strong. We endure because He is faithful.

Freedom means choosing not to go back, even when going back would be easier.

Standing in the Fire, Unshaken

In the book of Daniel, three young Hebrew men, Shadrach, Meshach, and Abednego, found themselves at a defining crossroads. Exiled in Babylon, they were commanded by King Nebuchadnezzar to bow down to a massive golden idol or face death in a fiery furnace. They didn't blink.

Their response is a courageous declaration:

> If we are thrown into the blazing furnace, the God we serve is able to deliver us from it… But even if He does not, we want you to know… we will not serve your gods.
>
> —Daniel 3:17-18 (emphasis added)

They believed God could save them, but they didn't make their faith conditional on the outcome. They were thrown into the fire fully clothed and fully committed. And what happened next was a miracle:

> "…Did we not cast three men bound into the midst of the fire?"… "Look!" he answered, "I see four men loose, walking in the midst of the fire…and the form of the fourth is like the Son of God.
>
> —Daniel 3:24-25 (NKJV)

God didn't only keep them from the fire, He joined them in it. They walked out untouched, unsinged, and unbound. It was a public testimony that God is with those who stand with Him.

Their story shows us that freedom is not the absence of heat; it's the presence of God in the middle of it. True perseverance says, "Even if He doesn't deliver me the way I hope, I will not bow."

The Gift of Endurance

Perseverance isn't just about gritting your teeth and trying harder. It's a gift of grace. It's the Holy Spirit strengthening your spirit.

It's the result of hope that refuses to die. Freedom to persevere means we don't live by what we feel. Instead, we live by what we know.

And we know:

- God is faithful. (2 Thessalonians 3:3)
- The results are coming. (Galatians 6:9)
- Our labor in the Lord is never in vain. (1 Corinthians 15:58)

We don't give up, and it's not because we're strong, but because we're held.

Don't Quit Before the Breakthrough

Some of the most powerful breakthroughs occur after we have almost given up. Weariness is a real thing. But so is the reward.

When you keep loving, forgiving, praying, sowing, giving, and showing up, you're planting seeds that will bear fruit in due season. Don't let the enemy convince you to quit in chapter ten of your story when God's already written chapter twelve. You have the freedom to endure. You have the freedom to wait with expectation. You have the freedom to believe even when the timeline doesn't make sense. God is still writing your story. And if He's not done, neither are you.

Reflection Questions

1. Where in your life are you tempted to give up, and what is God saying about that situation?

2. How does Joseph's story encourage you in seasons of waiting or injustice?

3. What lies try to surface when perseverance becomes difficult?

4. How can you draw strength from God's promises when the road is long?

5. What results are you believing God for, and how can you remain faithful in the meantime?

Notes

13

THE DESTINATION OF FREEDOM: HOLINESS AND ETERNAL LIFE

Dear friends, now we are children of God, and what we will be has not yet been made known. But we know that when Christ appears, we shall be like him, for we shall see him as he is.
—1 John 3:2

Every journey has a destination, and the destination of our freedom is to live eternal lives, not just to live better lives. It's not just to be changed, but to be with Jesus, fully and forever. This is the great promise that anchors everything we've walked through so far.

We began with chains we didn't always recognize: sin, shame, fear, striving. And as we surrendered to Christ, those chains started to fall. We learned to walk not in our strength, but in His Spirit. We found the courage to draw near to God with confidence. We set aside the opinions of others and adopted the identity He gave us. We embraced transformation, even when it was painful. We served, we loved, we forgave, we persevered.

And through it all, something deeper was happening: we were becoming more like Him. The Spirit was shaping us for a glorious future yet to be unveiled.

This glorious future isn't just about things getting better down here. It's about where all of this is headed. One day, we'll be fully with Jesus. The fight against sin will be over. The questions will be answered. The healing will be complete. And the work God has been doing in us all along will finally be finished. We won't just be trying to imagine Him by faith anymore. We'll see Him face to face.

Every act of obedience.

Every moment of surrender.

Every tear wiped in secret.

Every "yes" when no one else saw it.

All of it was leading us here to liberty in the presence of the Almighty God.

A Glimpse of the Destination: Stephen's Final Vision

If you've ever wondered what it looks like to finish the race well, look at Stephen. He was one of the early deacons of the Church, full of wisdom and the Holy Spirit. He boldly preached about Jesus in front of religious leaders who rejected the gospel. As they grew enraged at his words and rushed toward him to kill him, he wasn't looking at their faces; he was looking toward Heaven.

> But Stephen, full of the Holy Spirit, looked up to Heaven and saw the glory of God, and Jesus standing at the right hand of God, "Look," he said, "I see heaven open and the Son of Man standing at the right hand of God."
>
> —Acts 7:55-56

He was the first martyr of the Church, and what a gift that he didn't die looking at his enemies, but looking at Jesus. And Jesus wasn't sitting—He was standing, as if to rise in honor. As if to say: "You've made it. I see you. Welcome home."

Stephen died in peace. With glory in his eyes. With eternity in his lungs. He saw what we're all walking toward. His final moments weren't just about how he died, but they were about how he lived. He was a man who had been set apart, filled with the Spirit, bold in truth, and deeply surrendered. His eyes were already fixed on Jesus long before that day. And when the end came, there was no panic. There was only presence.

That's what a life of holiness produces: a soul already oriented toward Heaven and a life fully prepared to meet the One it has been pursuing all along. The apostle Paul wrote,

> But now that you have been set free from sin and have become slaves of God, the benefit you reap leads to holiness, and the result is eternal life.
>
> —Romans 6:22

The arc of our journey moves through being set free from sin, belonging to God, and walking in holiness until we enter into eternal life with Him. Holiness, which is not a burden, is the natural outcome of being united with Christ. It is the shaping of our character into His likeness, and the slow, steady transformation of our hearts, minds, and desires until they reflect His.

We Shall See Him as He Is

Right now, we live by faith. And faith, though powerful, is often mysterious. It's trusting in a God we cannot see. It's loving a Savior whose voice we hear internally. It's believing in promises we cannot yet touch. This is the blessed tension of the Christian life:

> Blessed are those who have not seen and yet have believed.
>
> —John 20:29b

Think about that. God is invisible. We don't see His face when we pray. We can't reach out and hold His hand (at least, not yet). Faith is what bridges that gap.

And if you're honest, you know what it's like to wrestle there, to long for more clarity, more certainty, more proof. To cling to unseen truth when your emotions are frayed. To trust in the dark. But one day, faith will no longer be necessary because on that day our faith will become sight.

> For now we see only a reflection as in a mirror; then we shall see face to face. Now I know in part; then I shall know fully, even as I am fully known.
>
> —1 Corinthians 13:12

No more imagining. No more wondering what He looks like. No more trying to picture His eyes, or His smile, or the tone of His voice. You will see Him with clarity. With certainty. With unfiltered glory. And when you do, all the wrestling, all the waiting, all the nights you held on by a thread will be worth it.

You'll see the One you prayed to in tears. The One you worshiped when you felt nothing. The One you believed in when the questions were louder than the answers. You will see Jesus.

And not just see Him, you will see Him as He is, in His fullness—His majesty, without measure, His holiness, without veils, His love, without question. Every doubt will disappear. Every scar will make sense. Every sacrifice will seem small in the presence of His glory. And in that one eternal moment, you'll know it was all worth it.

The Prisoner's Final Freedom

Remember the prisoner we've been journeying with? He once sat in a cold, dim cell, rightly condemned. Decisions, disappointments, addictions, and regrets had built the walls around him. The chains felt familiar. Freedom seemed meant for someone else.

Then, one day, a pardon was signed. The news reached his cell, almost too good to believe. He had lived under guilt for so long that he barely recognized the sound of grace. Yet a small whisper inside said, "Maybe it's true," so he stepped toward the gate. It opened, not with force, but with welcome. And so, he walked.

At first, the steps were slow. Freedom felt foreign. Shame tried to pull him back. Doubts about his worth pressed in. But he kept going. Along the way, old patterns gave way to a new identity. The opinions of others lost their power as God's voice grew louder. He learned to rest, to receive, to be still. He dared to love and be loved. Serving became joy. Transformation took root. Forgiveness flowed first to others, then to himself. Perseverance replaced quitting. Strength came through surrender. It wasn't a perfect walk, but it was free.

Like us, he lived each day with the greater hope in view, knowing that one day, the freedom he enjoyed on earth would give way to the fullness of freedom in Heaven. His journey through life was marked by grace, sustained by faith, and fueled by the promise that his destination was not a return to the life he once knew but entrance into the life he was always meant for.

Now, the road ends here. He is no longer a prisoner trying to believe he's free. He is a son, welcomed home—not to society, but into eternity. Ahead, the gates of Heaven stand open. And there, waiting, is the One who paid for his release.

Jesus is not seated—He's standing, just as He did for Stephen. Arms open. Smile radiant. Eyes filled with recognition. In that moment, everything makes sense. Every mile. Every tear. Every battle. Every scar.

He falls to his knees in awe. Failures are forgotten in the flood of love. The past has no voice here. Guilt is gone. Righteousness clothes him. Face to face, he meets the One who called him worthy when he felt worthless. The One who never left when doubt crept in. The One who walked beside him in silence and storms. The One who whispered, "You're free," long before he believed it. Now he knows he was never just walking toward a place, he was walking toward a Person.

And this Person is Jesus Christ.

This is the reward. It's not just freedom from the past, but eternal life with Jesus. It's not just release from guilt, but the fullness of joy in His presence. It's not just a new start, but a glorious finish.

This is the hope we live for.

The hope that sustains every step.

The hope that makes the journey worth it.

And it's a hope worth telling the world about.

Reflection Questions

1. What part of your freedom journey has shaped you most deeply?

2. How does the thought of seeing Jesus face to face stir your heart today?

3. In what ways are you pursuing holiness? How is God forming Christ in you?

4. Do you see yourself as that prisoner-turned-son or daughter? What emotions does that image stir?

5. Think of someone who needs to hear that freedom leads somewhere beautiful. How can your story point them there?

Notes

14

FREEDOM TO TELL YOUR STORY

And they overcame him by the blood of the Lamb and by the word of their testimony...
—Revelation 12:11

When you begin to grasp the destination of freedom (holiness, purpose, and eternal life in God), something begins to shift inside. The chains don't just fall off; they stay off. You no longer see yourself as disqualified or hidden, but as a living testimony of what God can do.

And when that realization takes root, a new freedom arises: the freedom to tell your story. Not a polished version. Not a perfect one. But the honest, grace-soaked, Spirit-empowered testimony of someone who has been set free.

One of the greatest gifts of walking freely in Christ is the ability to speak boldly about what He has done. When we've truly been set free from sin, shame, people-pleasing, fear, and self, we no longer feel bound to keep silent. Our lives become the message. Our story becomes our song.

Too often, we assume that our story has to be dramatic to be worth sharing. We hear testimonies of people rescued from addiction, prison, or extreme darkness and quietly compare our own. But every story of salvation is a miracle!

Whether Christ saved you from the gutter or self-righteousness, your story reveals God's grace in a way only you can tell it. You might think, "I'm still working through things," and that's okay. Your testimony isn't just about what God saved you from; it's also about what He's still transforming in you now. Sometimes, the most powerful stories are the unfinished ones. They invite others into hope.

Your Story Is Sacred

Throughout this journey, we've returned to the image of a prisoner declared free. Even before he realized it, his name was cleared. The cell door unlocked. His status changed. He wasn't instantly polished or perfect. He had to walk out his freedom, step by step. He had to leave behind old habits, navigate relationships, and learn to live in light of what had been declared over him.

In 2 Corinthians 3:2-3, Paul said:

> You yourselves are our letter, written on our hearts, known and read by everyone…written not with ink but with the Spirit of the living God.
>
> —2 Corinthians 3:2-3

You are the letter. Your life in Christ is living proof. It's not about having the right words. It's about being willing to shine the light of what Jesus has done in your life.

The Spirit Makes You a Witness

When Jesus promised His disciples power from on high, it wasn't just so they could perform miracles or preach eloquently; it was also so they could bear witness to the truth. He said:

> But you will receive power when the Holy Spirit comes on you; and you will be my witnesses…
>
> —Acts 1:8

That word "witness" is key. A witness simply tells what they've seen and experienced. No embellishment. No exaggeration. Just the truth of what Christ has done. Whether you're telling a friend over coffee, posting something online, or praying for someone in need, your story speaks. And the Holy Spirit empowers you to share it in ways that will reach hearts only you can touch.

Your Story Builds Community

In Acts 9, when Saul of Tarsus became Paul, many were hesitant to welcome him. His past was too loud. His story was too extreme. But then came Barnabas, a believer willing to vouch for the work of God in Paul's life.

Your story might still carry some echo of your past, but it doesn't define you. It qualifies you. It positions you to be a voice of hope for others who think they're too far gone. When you speak up, others discover they're not alone. Your freedom helps birth theirs. Your honest, courageous testimony helps the Church grow, and that testimony does not have to be perfect.

Unfinished but Transformed

The power of your testimony isn't just in how bad things were—it's in how faithful God has been. You don't need a dramatic "before and after" to glorify Jesus. All you need is a real encounter with Him.

Remember that prisoner we've been walking with. His story has reached its eternal reward, but ours is still being written. We're still on the road, still learning, still surrendering, still persevering. We carry the same freedom he discovered and the same hope he lived for, but now we're entrusted with the privilege of telling others about it.

Our past doesn't vanish, but it gets reframed by grace. The scars remain, yet they speak of healing. And when our lives are held up to the light of Christ, even those who once doubted can't deny the change. We were that prisoner. Former captives. Current witnesses. Ongoing miracles.

Zacchaeus climbed a tree to see Jesus, but left the encounter so transformed that he began making restitution to those he had wronged. Peter denied Jesus in His hour of need, but after grace restored him, he stood in Jerusalem and preached with power, leading thousands to faith. Stephen, full of the Spirit, spoke truth even as stones flew, forgiving his accusers and seeing Jesus standing to receive him. They were all different people with different pasts who encountered the same Savior and the same transforming power.

This is what it means to walk freely. We're no longer in hiding, but in the light, unashamed of the journey and confident in the One who walks with us, works in us, and will one day welcome us home.

Why Your Story Matters

We live in a world that's desperate for hope but skeptical of empty words. People may argue with doctrine, but they can't argue with a changed life. Your story is living proof that Jesus still saves, still heals, and still transforms.

When you share your story, you're not promoting yourself—you're putting the grace of God on display. You're saying, "This is who I was, this is who He is, and this is who I'm becoming because of Him." It doesn't have to be eloquent. It doesn't have to answer every theological question. It just has to be real.

Overcoming the Fear to Speak

For some, sharing their story feels natural. For others, it's terrifying. Maybe you're afraid people will judge you. Perhaps you don't think your story is "good enough." But the truth is, your story is about Him. It's not about you.

Think of the man in Mark 5 who had been possessed by demons. After Jesus set him free, he begged to go with Him. But Jesus sent him home with one assignment:

> Go home to your own people and tell them how much the Lord has done for you, and how he has had mercy on you.
>
> —Mark 5:19

That man became a walking testimony in his own community, and the people marveled.

Your freedom was never meant to be silent. You may never stand on a platform or hold a microphone, but every conversation, every act of kindness, every moment of honesty is an opportunity to point someone to Jesus.

Your Story, His Glory

Walking freely isn't just about living without chains—it's about using that freedom to glorify the One who set you free. It's about being willing to be vulnerable so others can see His power. It's about carrying the hope of glory in a world starving for it.

So, tell your story. Not just the before or the after, but the ongoing middle where His grace meets your weakness and His strength carries you forward. And when your road finally ends, like the prisoner's, your testimony will have been a beacon that pointed others toward the same Savior who welcomed you home.

Let this be your declaration:

God is real.

Jesus saves.

Grace works.

Freedom is possible.

And I am living proof.

Don't keep that to yourself!

Reflection Questions

1. How has your understanding of your story changed as you've walked through this book?

2. What are the key moments or truths in your journey with Christ that could encourage someone else?

3. Do you struggle with feeling like your story is too small or too messy? Why?

4. Who in your life needs to hear about the freedom God is working in you?

5. How can you begin to share your story—in conversation, writing, prayer, or public testimony—as an act of worship?

Notes

15

FREEDOM TO BE STILL AND KNOW

Be still, and know that I am God.
—Psalm 46:10a

As we tell our stories and bear witness to the freedom we've received, we must also remember that our testimony isn't sustained by constant activity—it's fueled by abiding in Him. We speak boldly, but we also rest deeply. The same God who calls us to go into the world also calls us to come away with Him. The journey of walking freely is not only about what we do for Christ, but about learning to be still and know that He is God.

The Stillness That Is Alive

There is a kind of stillness that is not passive, not empty, not apathetic, but deeply alive. It is the stillness of a soul anchored in the unshakable truth of who God is.

To be still and know God is to rest in the reality that He is God and we are not. It is to stop striving to earn what has already been given. It is to quiet the noise of fear, doubt, and distraction so we can hear His voice.

The One who calmed the storm with a word can calm the storm inside you. The One who fed the multitudes can meet your every need. The One who touched the leper is not afraid of your scars. Stillness is not withdrawal from life; it is stepping into life with the full awareness that you are held.

Freedom in Stillness

We've walked through several dimensions of spiritual freedom together, including freedom from sin, shame, people's opinions, the past, and even forgiving ourselves. We've seen how Christ's death and resurrection opened the door to an entirely new Spirit-filled life marked by transformation, identity, purpose, perseverance, and grace.

Freedom in Christ reaches its highest expression not always in movement, but in the kind of stillness that doesn't come from escape, but from surrender. It is the calm within the storm, the quiet confidence that comes from knowing who holds our lives.

Jesus: The Perfect Example

Stillness is not weakness. It's not passivity. It's not the absence of action. It's the presence of constant intentional trust. Jesus embodied this freedom perfectly. He lived on earth with unshakable assurance and was never anxious to prove Himself or rushed by human expectations. Whether teaching crowds, retreating to pray, confronting hypocrisy, or resting in the middle of a storm, His every step flowed from the confidence of knowing the Father intimately.

And now, that same confidence is available to us. Through His death and resurrection, Jesus removed every barrier that kept us at a distance from God. We are not left guessing what He is like. Instead, we can know His heart for ourselves. This is the freedom the gospel offers: the ability to come to God without fear, without pretense, without shame.

To know God is to be truly free from the exhausting attempts to earn His approval, from the distorted images of Him shaped by our past, and from the lie that He is far away and unreachable. Because of Jesus, we can approach Him boldly, hear His voice, and walk in step with His Spirit. This is the kind of freedom that changes how you live, pray, rest, and love. And it is the freedom Jesus died to give you.

We no longer have to hustle for approval. We don't need to carry guilt as if it were part of our identity. The door is open. The invitation is clear:

> Therefore, since we have a great high priest…let us then approach God's throne of grace with confidence…
>
> —Hebrews 4:14-16

Seeing God as He Truly Is

Freedom liberates us from sin and our misconceptions about God. Many of us have unknowingly worshipped an idea of Him shaped more by our wounds than by His Word. We carry images of a harsh judge, a distant ruler, or an impossible standard.

But Jesus came to show us the Father's heart. He is a God who is merciful, gracious, abounding in love, and faithful through every season. Freedom means we no longer have to see Him through the lens of shame or religion, but through the lens of Christ.

Like Moses, who dared to ask, "Show me Your glory."

Like David, who longed to dwell in the house of the Lord all his days.

Like Mary, who chose to sit at Jesus' feet while others scrambled to perform.

Like John, who leaned on Jesus' chest as a beloved friend.

Freedom offers salvation, and revelation, along with the right to know God's character, His voice, and His heart for each of us.

The Ongoing Journey

Freedom is a journey. Like Jonah, we wrestle with surrender. Like Peter, we fall into fear and regret. Like Zacchaeus, we carry reputations that feel hard to shake. Like Joseph, we endure hardship and wonder whether God has forgotten us. Like Paul, we press forward through affliction with only grace to keep us standing.

And yet, grace is enough. Always enough.

You may still feel like the prisoner we imagined earlier in this book—someone declared free, yet learning to walk in it. Transformation is not instant, but it is real. Step by step, God renews your mind, restores your heart, and rewrites your story.

The Rhythm of Grace

Even now, He is inviting you:

- Not to do more, but to rest
- Not to strive, but to surrender
- Not to perform, but to receive

This is the rhythm of grace: we sit before we walk. We listen before we speak. We are loved before we lift a finger.

> You will keep in perfect peace those whose minds are steadfast, because they trust in you.
>
> —Isaiah 26:3

This peace doesn't come from having all the answers, but from knowing the One who does. It's the assurance that He is faithful when we are frail, strong when we are broken, and present when we feel alone.

The Final Invitation

The same Jesus who said, "Come to Me…and I will give you rest," still calls today. If you have not yet made Him the Lord and Savior of your life, this is your moment. You don't have to earn it. You don't have to fix yourself first. Freedom begins with a "yes" and a willingness to surrender to the One who gave everything for you.

He has already pronounced you free.

He has already paid the debt.

Now, will you walk with Him?

If that is your desire, pray this prayer:

> *"Jesus, I believe You are the Son of God and that You gave Your life to set me free. Thank You for breaking the chains of my sin, my shame, and my past. I receive Your grace and lay down my striving, my fear, and my need for control. Teach me to walk in Your Spirit, to love without fear, to forgive freely, and to live for Your glory. I surrender my life, my heart, my will, and my future to You. Be my Savior, my Lord, and my constant freedom. Today I choose to walk freely with You, until the day I see You face to face. In Jesus' name, amen."*

This is the call of the gospel. This is the invitation of grace. This is what it means to walk freely. And in the stillness of that surrender, you will know that He is God.

And you will never be the same.

And for those already walking in that freedom, the call remains: be still, know that He is God, and walk freely until the day faith becomes sight.

Reflection Questions

1. Are past experiences, traditions, or fears shaping how you see God and hindering your ability to rest in His freedom?

2. In what areas of your life do you feel pressure to perform or the need for approval?

3. Do you approach God with confidence or hesitation? Why?

4. Which biblical character from this chapter do you relate to most, and what does their story reveal about God's grace in weakness?

5. What truth about God's character do you want to know more deeply in your heart?

Notes

ABOUT THE AUTHOR

John P. Martin is a pastor, teacher, and spiritual mentor with over two decades of ministry experience rooted in biblical teaching, discipleship, and compassionate leadership.

As the founder of The LifeHouse Ministries, John is recognized for his engaging, illustrative teaching style and his heart for helping people discover their identity and purpose in Christ.

John's journey of faith began in New York, where he was first called to ministry as a teenager. Since then, he has faithfully served in various roles, including youth pastor, associate pastor, and chaplain. His ministry is shaped by his miraculous personal testimony, theological depth, and a deep conviction that the grace of God can rewrite anyone's story.

He holds a Master of Theology and Ministry and has completed chaplaincy training through Duke University Hospital, continuing to provide pastoral care in both church and community settings.

Now based in North Carolina, John continues to equip believers to walk in the freedom Christ has already secured. He is a devoted husband to recording artist Rachel Martin, and together, they are raising their three children, Victoria, Noah, and Lily, to love God and serve others.

Walk Freely is both a reflection of Pastor John's teaching ministry and an invitation to experience lasting transformation through the power of God's grace.

Visit walkfreelytoday.com or email john@walkfreelytoday.com for booking inquiries or to connect with John.

www.ingramcontent.com/pod-product-compliance
Lightning Source LLC
LaVergne TN
LVHW091059150826
845673LV00002B/639

* 9 7 9 8 2 3 4 0 2 2 2 7 1 *